*Selected Epigrams*

Publication of this volume has been made possible, in part,

through the generous support and enduring vision of

Warren G. Moon.

# Selected Epigrams

# MARTIAL

Translated with notes by
# Susan McLean

The University of Wisconsin Press

The University of Wisconsin Press
1930 Monroe Street, 3rd Floor
Madison, Wisconsin 53711-2059
uwpress.wisc.edu

3 Henrietta Street, Covent Garden
London WC2E 8LU, United Kingdom
eurospanbookstore.com

Printed in the United States of America

Library of Congress Cataloging-in-Publication Data
Martial, author.
[Epigrammata. Selections. English]
Selected epigrams / Martial; translated with notes by Susan McLean.
pages       cm — (Wisconsin studies in classics)
Includes bibliographical references and index.
ISBN 978-0-299-30174-3 (pbk.: alk. paper)
ISBN 978-0-299-30173-6 (e-book)
1. Martial—Translations into English.
2. Epigrams, Latin—Translations into English.
I. McLean, Susan, 1953–, translator.   II. Title.
III.  Series: Wisconsin studies in classics.
PA6502.M37       2014
878′.0102—dc23
2014007450

# Contents

# Contents

# *Preface*

Who was Martial? He was a talented poet with a particular genius for humor, wit, and satire. He was also an outsider of modest means from a distant province in what is now Spain. He came to Rome as a young man hoping to earn a living from writing, which could be done only by finding wealthy patrons. The contradictions between his skills and his goals were many. Readers enjoyed satiric and humorous verse, but ranked it very low among forms of literature. Satire was also dangerous. Satiric poets ran the risk of alienating patrons if the patrons suspected that they were butts of the satire. Although the emperor was the most desirable patron of all, since he could provide the greatest rewards, prominent writers such as Seneca, Petronius, and Lucan had been forced to commit suicide when they had angered their ruling emperor, Nero.

Martial's response to these challenges was pragmatic. To the dangerous emperor Domitian, he offered poems of hyperbolic flattery. Martial seems to have been largely disappointed in his hopes of generous reward from Domitian. Although he did survive that ruler's fifteen-year-long reign, he later found that his praise of Domitian did not ingratiate him with subsequent emperors. He also flattered a large number of lesser patrons, writing poems in praise of them and often addressing them in poems as friends who would concur with his satirical gibes at others. Unlike Catullus, whose satirical epigrams Martial admired, Martial publicly insisted that his satire was not directed at real individuals. Other than patrons, real people named in his satirical poems were already safely dead. From his patrons Martial received enough income to qualify for the privileges of a knight and to support his taste for good wine, good food, and attractive slave boys. He did not, however, achieve the kind of financial independence that would free him from the onerous duties of paying morning calls on patrons (as he often complained) until he finally retired to his hometown in Spain near the end of his life.

To write effective satirical epigrams, a writer needs a keen sense of the ridiculous, incisive wit, and trenchant punch lines. In addition to these skills, Martial had insight into the quirks of human behavior, and a delight in bawdy humor. Since many of Martial's poems are putdowns of one kind or another, one might assume that he had a malicious or sour personality. But the poems themselves provide contrary evidence. His tender epitaphs for child slaves, such as Erotion (5.34) and Pantagathus (6.52), his poems in praise of balance and moderation in life (5.20; 10.47), and his poems that poke fun at himself (6.82; 10.9) all reveal a man who combined wit with feeling and who was as ready to laugh at himself as at others.

As Freud points out in *Jokes and Their Relation to the Unconscious*, humor often has a sexual or aggressive element in it (97). Because these impulses must normally be repressed in social interactions, humor provides pleasure, both for the person telling the joke and for those laughing at it, by enabling the impulse to be expressed despite the social taboos against it (100–101) and by providing temporary relief from the psychic energy used to maintain the repression (118). Freud notes that "innocent" jokes, which lack this element of violating taboos, seldom cause a burst of laughter (96). Martial, when satirizing an unnamed writer of bland and innocuous epigrams (7.25) or an epigrammatist whose language and subjects are always chaste (3.69), implies that such approaches just aren't entertaining. His use of generic names for the targets of his satire allows Martial to make jokes about even the rich and powerful, because he can do so without making his emperor or patrons think that he is attacking them. In a joke about a generic target, no individual gets hurt. Martial is thus able both to enjoy rebellion against authority figures and, by satirizing those who violate the standards of acceptable behavior in society, to align himself with those in power, using embarrassment as a tool to maintain social codes.

It is difficult to winnow a clear notion of Martial's personality from the many stances he adopts for the sake of his jokes and satires. He visited and dined with the wealthy and powerful, but his dependent status meant he was not treated as one of them. He often jokes about his poverty, his mean apartment, his meager farm in Nomentum, and his threadbare toga, yet some of his complaints may have been intended as hints to patrons that more support was needed. He appears to be proud of his fame, irritated by plagiarists who try to claim his wit and skill for themselves, and unwilling to accept the general assessment that epigrams were a lesser form of literature than the odes, epics, and tragedies that people of his time valued more. Any dissatisfactions he had with his patrons had to be expressed as jokes and directed at pseudonymous targets in a way that wouldn't anger the actual patrons. Yet despite Martial's need to be circumspect in his writing, Pliny the Younger, who knew him, states in one of his published letters (3.21) that Martial had no less candor than wit and acerbity (236; my translation). Undoubtedly Martial was as complex and contradictory as most people, yet I have found in translating his poems that he comes across as a man with an irrepressible gusto for life and a fascination with human behavior in all its forms.

This translation of about a third of the Latin epigrams of Martial is meant to provide a wide cross section of Martial's satirical themes, subjects, and humorous and poetic techniques, in contemporary, colloquial language, for an audience of college students and general readers. The poems are translated into rhymed, metrical verse in an attempt to capture the poetic polish of the originals. I selected these epigrams to convey a vivid and varied portrait of Roman life in the first century CE, to show the range of Martial's tones and subjects, and to showcase his satirical wit and often racy humor. I tended to favor the shorter, funnier, and more accessible epigrams over longer ones (in which the final point often does not seem to be worth the long setup), those that are overfull of allusions to classical myth or history, those that are mainly intended to flatter patrons, those that depend on untranslatable puns, or those whose humor would not come across to contemporary readers. Some of Martial's humor depends on obscenity, which has often been avoided or minimized in past translations, and I have tried not to downplay that element, but have provided notes to explain jokes and attitudes that may seem puzzling to readers unfamiliar with Roman culture. Humor varies over time and between cultures; I have not tried to impose current standards of sensitivity on poems whose humor often may seem racist, sexist, offensive in its treatment of gay men, lesbians, and people with physical disabilities, or callous about violence toward and sexual abuse of slaves.

The Latin text on which these translations are based is the Loeb Classical Library edition of Martial by D. R. Shackleton Bailey (Cambridge, MA: Harvard University Press, 1993). I have chosen to omit the epigrams from Martial's first three collections: *De Spectaculis*, written to commemorate the games at the opening of the Flavian Amphitheater, later called the Colosseum; *Xenia*, two-line poems to accompany gifts of food and wine; and *Apophoreta*, two-line poems to accompany other gifts. Those three collections provide evidence of the kinds of shows presented at the arena and the kinds of gifts that would have been exchanged at the Saturnalia, but they hold limited interest for the contemporary reader, whereas the satire of human behavior contained in the main twelve books is perennially interesting and amusing, while also providing a lively and detailed view of life in ancient Rome.

Martial writes in a number of classical meters, particularly elegiac couplets (alternating lines of dactylic hexameter and dactylic pentameter, which make up the majority of his epigrams) and hendecasyllabics (lines of eleven syllables), but I have followed the customary practice of English translators in using English meters instead. Latin quantitative verse, which is based on patterns of long and short vowels, has very different rhythms than English accentual-syllabic verse, in which the patterns are created by stressed and unstressed syllables. A translator cannot simply substitute stresses for vowel length while maintaining the same patterns. Though some attempts to adapt classical meters to English have been made by poets such as Tennyson and Swinburne, the practice has not caught on, and for good reason. The rhythms of classical meters tend to sound odd and jerky in English; and the longer the poem is, the more monotonous the resulting pattern becomes. Dactylic meter, quite common in Latin, is rare and calls attention to itself in English; the vast majority of English poetry is written in iambic meter, which most closely approximates English speech rhythms and—with the help of common metrical substitutions—can sound both elegant and colloquial. I have therefore stuck to iambic meter in my translations. Latin words tend to have more syllables than English words, so an English translation of a Latin line will usually have fewer syllables but more words than the Latin.

Like most English translators of Martial, I have added rhymes to his poems, although classical Latin poems did not rhyme. Rhyme has for centuries been an essential feature of the epigram in English, adding surprise and wit to punch lines by bringing together dissimilar things in unexpected ways.

Rhyme also can add emphasis and closure in poems. Since English poetry does not have as many meters as Latin, rhyme adds an element of poetic craft that helps to convey the polish of Martial's poetry. Translators have most commonly resorted to rhymed couplets to convey Martial's wit, but having the rhymes come close together can make it hard to convey the poem's content accurately. For poems longer than two lines, I have preferred to rhyme every other line in order to gain flexibility and accuracy, sometimes using a couplet to provide more emphatic closure at the end.

I have tried to remain as close as possible to the length and number of lines of Martial's epigrams and to avoid omitting or adding material to the poems. For Martial's longer lines I tend to use iambic pentameter (five iambic feet), the most common meter in English, even when translating lines of hexameter (six feet), because hexameters tend to drag in English. When the content cannot be boiled down to a pentameter line, I have occasionally used heptameter lines (seven feet), which tend to be heard as alternating lines of tetrameter (four feet) and trimeter (three feet), a pattern common in English ballads and hymns. The heptameter lines can sound urbane, but the pentameter ones usually have more comic impact, so I use heptameter sparingly. On a few occasions, I have used one line of hexameter followed by a line of pentameter, in imitation of the elegiac couplet itself, but in iambic meter. For Martial's hendecasyllabics I often use iambic tetrameter (a sprightlier rhythm than pentameter), although I try to suit the rhythm to the poem's content, as well. Latin and Greek names, especially polysyllabic ones, can be hard to fit into the lines without making the lines quite long. I have retained the names wherever possible, but where both the satirical target and an addressee are named, I have often dropped one of the names, usually the addressee's. Though the addressees were real people and the targets were usually invented, the addressees are named as a compliment to a patron, whereas the names of targets are sometimes relevant to the content of the epigram. If the poem has an odd number of lines, instead of adding an extra line for the sake of the rhyme scheme, I have often resorted to alternate rhyme schemes or interlocking rhymes in order to avoid padding the lines with material not in the original.

Some translators update situations or Anglicize names in their translations in order to make Martial's epigrams seem more contemporary. I prefer to leave the poems in their own cultural context, but occasionally substitute a more common name for a lesser-known "poetic" term (Venus for Cytherea, for example) or add a compensatory gloss, filling in some details that would not have needed explaining for the original audience, in order to avoid the need for readers to consult the notes. I also substitute English idioms for Latin idioms instead of translating word for word, so that the colloquial flavor of Martial's language can be retained. I have tried to maintain the level of obscenity of Martial's language by finding equally obscene terms in English because the obscenity is part of the humor of the epigrams in question. Puns are usually untranslatable, and many of the sonic effects in the original wording cannot be re-created in another language; instead, I have tried to create equally musical effects using English. Because of the much larger vocabulary in English, I often have used synonyms instead of repeating the same word again, sometimes to gain variety, but more often to accommodate the demands of rhyming. In the cases in which Martial quotes a Greek phrase, I have translated it into English, too, since contemporary readers are even less likely to know Greek than to know Latin. Although in my notes I often refer to the speaker in the poems as "Martial," and many of his poems include autobiographical details that seem to be based on fact, other poems, such as those that refer to his "wife," seem to be written using a persona created for comic purposes, so readers should be cautious about assuming that any of the epigrams are straightforward autobiography or reflect the author's actual attitudes.

I wish to thank the editors of *Transference*, *Measure*, *Lucid Rhythms*, the *Classical Outlook*, *Blue Unicorn*, the *Chimaera*, *Amphora*, *Arion*, *Literary Imagination*, *Light Quarterly*, *Two Lines*, the *Formalist*, and the *Neovictorian/Cochlea*, in which some of these translations first appeared, often in earlier versions. I also wish to thank the University of Iowa, Cambridge University, the American Academy in Rome, and Southwest Minnesota State University for their research facilities, and John Finamore, Peter Green, Art L. Spisak, Dick Davis, John N. Drayton, and the anonymous reviewers of the manuscript for their suggestions. I owe A. M. Juster a special debt of gratitude for getting me interested in Martial in the first place, and D. R. Shackleton Bailey a much greater debt for the excellent help his literal translations and notes provided.

# Introduction
# A Life in Epigram

## Marc Kleijwegt

The ruins of Augusta Bilbilis are located 2.5 miles north of the modern city of Calatayud, which is 145 miles northeast of Madrid. In its heyday, the first and second century CE, Bilbilis was an impressive city overlooking the valley of the river Jalón from the heights of the Cerro de Bámbola; it boasted a forum, a main temple located on an immense podium, baths, and a theater.[1] The epithet Augusta suggests that the city was founded with the rank of a *municipium* in an unknown year after 27 BCE, the year in which the great-nephew of Julius Caesar was given the honorary name Augustus. The new foundation replaced a Celtiberian settlement, either on the same site or at Valdeherrera five miles to the southeast.[2] In a *municipium* local aristocrats could acquire Roman citizenship for themselves and their families by holding political office. Over time this strategy produced a pool of families who became more and more Roman in outlook, mentality, and cultural attitudes, and more loyal to the central seat of power. Its success can be inferred from the complete absence of Celtiberian names in the epigraphic record and from the lifestyle and the cultural worldview endorsed and promoted by the city's inhabitants. The houses and apartments that have been excavated since 2006 are richly decorated with

frescoes, an indication that the local population was eager to
share in a cultural language that originated from the main center
of political power. Bilbilis is the place of birth of Marcus Valerius
Martialis, better known as the poet Martial. With one important
exception that will be discussed at the end of this introduction,
all the information on Martial's life and his career as a writer
comes from his poetry.

The process of reconstructing Martial's life and career is an
inexact science. Some of the important moments in his life can
be pinpointed with confidence, but the poet's motivations are
beyond reconstruction. Consequently it is possible to mark the
year in which Martial went to Rome, but it is not possible to
identify his reasons for doing so. Martial never discusses them
and the best that can be done is to draw on better documented
cases of provincials who established themselves in the metropo-
lis.[3] Likewise, it is possible to identify the moment when Martial
returned to Spain, but it is hard to determine what made him
take this step. This time his poetry offers a number of clues that
suggest that he had become dissatisfied with the life of a client
in the big city. While some scholars believe that this provides a
satisfactory explanation for his decision to return to Bilbilis,
others argue that the political circumstances of the time were
influential as well. Martial never mentions the political changes
following the assassination of Domitian in September of 96 as
a factor in his decision to return to Spain.

The study of other facets of Martial's life runs into prob-
lems of a different kind. Martial writes his poetry from a first
person perspective, an annotator on society who condemns and
endorses particular forms of behavior. Altogether, the expres-
sions and opinions communicated by the epigrams constitute
an interesting window on the social, sexual, and ideological
values of Rome in the final two decades of the first century.
They do not, however, constitute the (or even a) reality, nor
do they form the private views of the poet Martial.[4] This is
supported by Martial himself. He proclaims that his use of

straightforward language on matters of sexuality should not be
taken to mean that his life is equally rugged and rough: "my
page is wanton, but my life is virtuous" (1.4.8).[5] The "I" of the
poems is a *persona*, a personality or character that is adopted for
the occasion of a poem or a series of poems.[6] Martial is the
master of multiple *personae*, sometimes occupying conflicting
positions within the same book of epigrams. There exists no
reliable strategy, historical, philological, or otherwise, that en-
ables the reader to distinguish successfully between the multiple
identities in Martial's poetry and to declare one of them to be
the true voice of the poet (not in the literal sense in which this
expression is commonly used). This problem becomes immedi-
ately relevant when Martial's education and his domestic life are
examined.

Martial was of Celtiberian descent (4.55; 7.52; 10.65 [page
83]). The names of his parents, however, are undeniably Ro-
man: Fronto and Flaccilla (5.34 [page 44]).[7] From this it can be
inferred that one of Martial's ancestors must have received
Roman citizenship by holding municipal office. A line from a
later epigram reveals that Martial's parents had him taught
grammar and rhetoric (9.73.7).[8] It is uncertain where this
training could have taken place. The number of options are
limited: in Bilbilis or in a larger city in the same region such as
Caesaraugusta (Zaragoza) or Tarraco (Tarragona).[9] There is
disagreement between scholars whether Martial's access to
higher education suggests that his parents were comfortably
off (Watson and Watson 1) or whether it is useless as an indica-
tion of the status of the family of the poet (Henriksén 90). It is
hard to imagine, however, that access to rhetorical training, in
whatever form, was commonly available at a level below that of
the municipal elite. It is obvious, then, that Martial received a
decent education, although it needs to be pointed out that the
traditional upper-class education would have involved an ap-
prenticeship with an experienced orator. This was also available
to provincials as can be inferred from the case of Martial's fellow

Spaniard Quintilian (born in 35), from Calagurris, a town of roughly the same size and importance as Bilbilis. He left his hometown as a teenager to train with Cn. Domitius Afer (who was from Nîmes in southern Gaul) in the early 50s of the first century.[10] It is not certain why Martial did not follow the same path. He may not have been as talented as Quintilian, or not as ambitious, or his parents may have lacked the necessary social connections to place him in an apprenticeship.

Most scholars argue that Martial never married.[11] This idea has been challenged from time to time, most recently by Patricia and Lindsay Watson (Watson; Watson and Watson 3).[12] The point of departure for their argument is the fact that Martial petitioned successive Flavian emperors for the *ius trium liberorum*, a privilege that was a reward for women who had delivered three (or more) children (four for freedwomen).[13] Martial claims to have received the privilege on two different occasions (see 3.95.5: *Caesar uterque*; "both Caesars"), which may be a reference to Titus and Domitian. It is uncertain what his marital status was on each occasion. There are three options available, of which the most obvious one—that he was married and had three children—has not been defended by any scholar. Of the remaining two options the first one is supported by external evidence (but not by Martial) and the second by Martial (but for which there is no parallel). The privilege could have been granted as compensation for an infertile marriage or it could have been the result of recognition of a talented writer.[14] For his active career as a poet—roughly from 83 to 101—it is impossible to determine whether he was married or not because of Martial's use of different personae. In many epigrams he refers to a wife or, to put it somewhat differently, he develops a scenario in which the speaker of the poem is married (2.90; 2.92 [page 22]; 3.92; 4.24 [page 35]; 7.95; 11.43 [page 89]; 11.104), but in other cases the speaker is clearly not married (2.49 [page 17]; 8.12 [page 63]; 10.8 [page 78]; 11.19 [page 88]; 11.23). The confusion is greatest in book 11, where Martial refers to a wife in two cases but also identifies himself as unmarried in the same number of epigrams.

In an epigram that is extremely important for the reconstruction of Martial's biography, the poet is celebrating his fifty-seventh birthday (10.24). Establishing a precise date for the poem enables the reader to discover the year in which Martial was born. The tenth book as we have it today was published in 98, some two years after the assassination of Domitian and within a year after the death of his successor Nerva.[15] An earlier version had been published at the beginning of 96 or the final part of 95, but in September of 96 the emperor Domitian was assassinated and this forced the poet to withdraw the original publication and to publish a revised edition two years later.[16] In 10.2 Martial announces that the majority of the epigrams are new and that others have been substantially revised. Sullivan (*Martial* 46) argues that as many as twenty-five or thirty poems on Domitian may have been excised and that they were replaced with poems honoring Nerva and Trajan (10.6; 10.7; 10.34; 10.72) and poems dealing with the nuisance of plagiarism (10.3; 10.5; 10.80 [page 84]; 10.100 [page 86]). Scholars hesitate whether the poem in which Martial celebrates his birthday already formed part of the first publication or whether it was one of the epigrams newly written for the second edition.[17] It is logical, however, to assume that when it first appeared, book 10 was organized like any other of Martial's books of epigrams, brandishing a mixture of praise of the emperor, cheeky exposure of misfits and miscreants, and lambasting comments on patrons for their unwillingness to provide financial support for the speaker. In its present format, book 10 differs substantially from any other book of Martial's epigrams. Hannah Fearnley (618) aptly describes it as the "only Martial book in which the poet stops and takes stock of his past and his future." It must be assumed that this was the result of the modifications required by the changes in the political landscape and this implies that 10.24 was not part of the original publication of

96.[18] It is therefore overly cautious to argue that Martial's year of birth is uncertain; 41 is by far the most likely candidate.

In another epigram from book 10 Martial reveals that he had lived in Rome for thirty-four years (10.103.7). Since it has already been established that book 10 was published in 98, it can be concluded that the poet arrived in the capital in 64. The emperor at the time was Nero, who was then just twenty-six years old but already in the ninth year of his reign (Nero, who was born on 15 December 37, succeeded his adoptive father Claudius on 13 October 54; he was then sixteen years old). In the summer of 64 major parts of the inner city were destroyed by fire. Nero, who was at his villa in Antium when the fire broke out, rushed back to the capital and introduced measures to combat the fire, to aid the families of the victims, and to protect the city against major fires in the future (Tacitus, *Annals* 15.39). In the aftermath of the fire Nero started to build a magnificent new palace, which he named the *Domus Aurea*, "the Golden House." The complex was on such a grand scale that anonymous verses circulated recommending the population to move to Veii since all of Rome was occupied by a single house (Suetonius, *Life of Nero* 39.2). The hostility toward Nero's project is echoed in one of Martial's epigrams from his *Liber Spectaculorum* ("The Book of the Games"; 2.4). However, this poem was not written at the time the palace was being constructed but on the occasion of the opening of the Colosseum in 80, the building that replaced part of Nero's Golden House. Whenever Nero is referred to in the epigrams (4.63 [page 39]; 7.21 [page 58]; 7.34.4–5; 7.44; 7.45; 8.52; 8.70; 9.26; 10.48.4; 11.6.10), he is an item of the past. Two of the three immediate successors of Nero after his suicide in June of 68, Galba and Vitellius, fail to make an appearance in the epigrams. Otho is praised (6.32) for his suicide at Bedriacum, but the poem was presumably written in the early 90s when Otho's short spell as emperor seems to have received a more favorable interpretation.[19] Vespasian and Titus have no significant presence in the

twelve books of epigrams.[20] This leads to a problem of wider
significance for an understanding of Martial's career. There is
no trace of Martial's activities between his arrival in Rome and
the appearance of what is arguably his first published work (see
the discussion below), the *Xenia*, in 83/84 (for the date, see Leary,
*Xenia* 13). The scholarly tradition holds that he received a warm
welcome (and financial support) from fellow Spaniards and
used the period after his arrival to perfect the art of epigram.[21]

A writer's chances for literary success in Rome depended
on his ability to win over wealthy individuals who were willing
to sponsor literary activities. This was difficult enough for an
author born in Rome or Italy, but it was arguably even more
difficult for a poet who came from a relatively insignificant part
of the Roman Empire. In order to gain a foothold it is believed
that Martial contacted fellow Spaniards.[22] Seneca (born in 1
BCE) and his nephew Lucan from Cordoba (born in 39) have
been identified as the most likely candidates to act as sponsors
of the young poet. Seneca was a Stoic philosopher, a writer of
political and moral treatises and an influential political thinker.
In 49 Agrippina, freshly married to the emperor Claudius (her
uncle), orchestrated Seneca's return from exile on the island of
Corsica (where he had been sent because of an alleged adulter-
ous relationship with Livilla, Agrippina's sister) to become the
tutor of her son Domitius Ahenobarbus, the future emperor
Nero. When Seneca's student succeeded Claudius in 54 he con-
tinued to serve as his principal adviser. In that capacity he wrote
the emperor's speeches and coached (or at least tried to coach)
the young emperor to act in the tradition of Augustus. Lucan
is generally viewed as the most exciting poet of the Neronian
age. He made his debut at the first edition of the Neronia in
60 with a poem in honor of Nero (Suetonius, *Life of Lucan* 1;
Suetonius, *Life of Nero* 12.3). Soon after (although it is un-
known how soon) he gave public recitations of his major work,
the *Pharsalia*, a brilliant but politically incorrect epic poem on
the civil war between Caesar and Pompey. At the time when

Martial arrived in Rome, however, Seneca and Lucan had lost
much of their influence and could no longer serve as a secure
route to the financial and literary support of the most impor-
tant patron of all, the emperor himself. Seneca had retired from
his position as Nero's adviser in 62 to devote himself exclusively
to writing (Tacitus, *Annals* 14.52–56). Lucan had been subjected
to a publishing ban by the emperor, which is believed to have
been in place by the summer of 64.[23] Within a year of Martial's
arrival in Rome both were suspected of involvement in a con-
spiracy against the emperor and committed suicide.

   The fact that Lucan and Seneca were no longer on friendly
terms with Nero does not preclude the possibility that they
provided financial support to Martial. However, there is nothing
in Martial's poetry that provides solid evidence for such a rela-
tionship. The argument that Seneca and Lucan acted as Mar-
tial's patrons ultimately rests on a number of inferences. In two
poems (4.40; 12.36) Seneca is hailed as an important patron of
the arts, the kind of generous patron that is sadly missing from
imperial Rome under Domitian, who ruled from 81 to 96. All
patrons mentioned in 12.36 (Piso, Memmius, Seneca, Crispus)
appear in the plural, suggesting a generic ideal rather than a
cherished individual.[24] Another approach also comes up empty.
The tangible result of Seneca's support for Martial is thought to
have been an estate at Nomentum, a small town twenty miles
northeast of Rome. The Nomentan estate is already referred to
in the *Xenia* and the first two books of the epigrams (13.15;
13.42; 13.119; 1.105 [page 10]; 2.38 [page 16]), which means that
Martial's ownership of the estate can be safely assumed for the
early 80s. The assumption that the source of this estate was
Seneca is only supported by the circumstance that Seneca owned
property at Nomentum. This property was a vineyard, which,
by the evidence of the epigrams, Martial's estate was not.[25]

   The evidence for financial support from Lucan is slim. It
consists of a series of epigrams in book 7 that celebrates Lucan's
achievements on the occasion of his birthday (7.21 [page 58];

7.22; 7.23). Two of the poems are addressed to Lucan's widow
Polla Argentaria (7.21; 7.23), which suggests that she was the
individual who had commissioned them.[26] Martial's seventh
book was published in December of 92, and it is around the
same time that the poet Statius produced his poem in honor
of Lucan (*Silvae* 2.7).[27] The best explanation for this outpour-
ing of poetry is a specific event for which Polla Argentaria
approached several poets. The most likely date is 3 November
89, the day on which Lucan would have turned fifty.[28] In a
later epigram (10.64 [page 83]), which accompanies the gift of
a set of books of epigrams, Martial addresses Polla Argentaria
explicitly as a patron (10.64.1). This may be interpreted as an
attempt to continue a relationship that had not progressed
beyond the initial stages. After this there is only silence. It is clear
that Martial saw Polla Argentaria as one of his patrons, but
there is no evidence that this relationship continued beyond
the commissioned poems of 89.[29] There is also no evidence that
the relationship started in 64.[30]

Martial mentions several other wealthy and cultured
Spaniards in his epigrams, but none were in Rome when the
poet arrived in 64 and only one can be positively identified as a
possible patron. L. Valerius Licinianus from Bilbilis (1.49.3;
1.61.11–12) appears in three epigrams, all of which are addressed
to him (1.49.1–3; 1.61.11–12; 4.55.1).[31] The reference in one
poem to a type of shoes only worn by magistrates (1.49.31) can
be taken as a strong indication that he was a senator. It is highly
likely that Martial's Licinianus is the same person as the former
praetor Valerius Licinianus, who was exiled under Domitian
for entertaining immoral relations with a Vestal Virgin (Pliny
the Younger, *Letters* 4.11).[32] It is clear that Pliny's Licinianus
was a well-educated man who was regarded as one of the most
eloquent advocates in Rome (4.11.1). This matches Martial's
Licinianus, who is heralded as an individual who brings glory
to Bilbilis (1.61.11–12) and is praised as *laus nostrae Hispaniae*
(1.49.2: "glory of our Spain").[33] There is, however, no absolute

certainty that Licinianus was one of Martial's patrons, for no
specific instance of his generosity toward the poet is recorded.
Another native from Bilbilis who is certified to have been one
of Martial's frequent contacts in Rome is Maternus. It is not
possible to draw a positive conclusion on his identity.[34] The
two opening lines of the long epigram that is addressed to him
in Martial's tenth book praise him extensively as a legal expert
(10.37.1–2). He is addressed as an old friend (*veterique sodali*),
but there is no evidence that he played a supporting role in
Martial's early years in Rome or in the reign of Vespasian.[35]

    Another Spaniard who is frequently identified as a patron
of Martial is L. Licinius Sura from Tarraco.[36] Sura held his first
consulship in 97 under Nerva, which was followed by a second
(102) and a third (107) under Trajan.[37] The fact that he was
active as a general in the Dacian wars in the first decade of the
second century suggests that Sura was much younger than
Martial, perhaps by as much as twenty years. This means that
he was only an adolescent when Martial arrived in Rome. He is
mentioned in a passionate praise of his home country written
upon the occasion of Licinianus' return (see above) to Spain
(1.49.40), and in another from the sixth book he is referred to
as someone who reads and praises Martial's work (6.64.13).
However, this is not enough to list him "among the great pa-
trons of poets of his time" (as does Galán Vioque 292). An epi-
gram (7.47) written on the occasion of Sura's recovery from an
illness suggests that Martial sought him out as a patron in the
early 90s, but since there are no further epigrams addressed to
him after 7.47, the most obvious conclusion is that Martial's
attempt met with very little success.[38] The only individual of
Spanish background who can be securely identified as a patron
is Decianus from Emerita, an advocate (2.5.6 [page 13]) and a
disciple of Stoic philosophy (1.8.1–2). He features in many
poems in the first book of epigrams (1.24 [page 4]; 1.39; 1.61.10)
and is the dedicatee of the second book (2 pref.; 2.5 [page 13]),
which is a reliable sign that Decianus was one of Martial's

patrons, but he disappears from view after the second book. This has been taken to suggest that he passed away shortly after its publication or that the relationship was terminated for another reason.[39]

It remains difficult to sketch in Martial's activities from his arrival in Rome (64) to the publication of his first collection of epigrams (83). If he was already a poet by the time he arrived in Rome it is difficult to understand why his first collection of epigrams appeared only twenty years after his arrival. There are a number of possibilities. The conventional idea is that he wrote epigrams for patrons but did not publish them as part of a collection.[40] The main evidence for this is that Martial followed this particular strategy with the numbered books of epigrams that started to appear, roughly speaking, once every year from 86 onward.[41] Epigrams were written for specific occasions or at the request of a patron. After an intermission, sometimes lasting as many as three years, the poems were collected in a book and made available through booksellers. However, how certain is it that Martial already followed this strategy before 86? The idea is hard to substantiate, and it is therefore frequently supplemented with a discussion of two epigrams from the first book that suggest that Martial wrote poetry before 83. The first epigram (1.113 [page 12]: *Quaecumque lusi iuvenis et puer quondam / apinasque nostras, quas nec ipse iam novi*; "what I wrote in play / as a young man and boy once, you may seek it / (rubbish I hardly recognize today)") refers to poetry Martial wrote as a *iuvenis* ("young man") and a *puer* ("boy"; "child"). In another epigram from the same book (1.101) Martial mourns the passing of his editorial assistant whose handwriting was known to the Caesars, which is usually interpreted as a reference to Titus and Domitian (rather than to Vespasian and Titus).[42] It is possible that Martial wrote epigrams before 80, but that those poems have not survived. However, these two poems are not without problems of interpretation. For example, Martial was twenty-three years old when he arrived in Rome. A

Roman child remained a boy (*puer*) until he replaced his chil-
dren's toga with the toga of adulthood, and this customarily
happened between the ages of fourteen and eighteen. Poems
that Martial wrote as a boy must have been written while he
was still in school in Spain. It seems very unlikely that such
poems were for sale at the store of a bookseller in Rome, as
the remainder of 1.113 (page 12) would have it. The unwritten
assumption behind any attempt to fill in the gaps in Martial's
career between 64 and 83 is that he arrived in Rome as a talented
poet looking for a network of patrons and eager readers. That
may still be the most plausible reconstruction, but it remains a
problem that he only started to publish his poetry after 83. The
alternative is to assume that Martial only became a writer of
epigrams in Rome.[43]

The landscape of epigram (lit. "inscribed text") as it may
have appeared to Martial at the beginning of his career is that
of a well-developed genre with a strong Greek pedigree. The
literary genre of epigram arose in the third century BCE out of
the (by then already) longstanding practice of inscribing poems
on funerary tombs. Callimachus famously defined good poetry
on the basis of slimness rather than length, thereby flying in the
face of tradition, which gave pride of place to epic. Slimness
remained the rule for epigram for the remainder of its history,
a rule that Martial has fun breaking from time to time (1.110
[page 11]; 2.77; 3.83 [page 31]; 6.65; 10.59 [page 82]). Short
poems with a pungent punch line proved enormously popular
in the age of literary experimentation that was the Hellenistic
period. The first anthology was produced by Meleager of Gadara
around 95 BCE, followed by *The Garland of Philip*, which was
published in the reign of Nero and included poets from the
Augustan period. The genre became even more popular by the
influx into Rome of Greek poets, such as Philodemus of Gadara
and Antipater of Thessalonica, who adapted the genre to the
tastes and political reality of the Roman world.[44] Both poets
received financial support from L. Calpurnius Piso Caesoninus,

consul in 15 BCE and putatively identified as the owner of the Villa of the Papyri in Herculaneum.[45]

The establishment of the Principate in 27 BCE provided further opportunities for the development of the genre and its practitioners. Greek writers of epigram had not sought out rulers of the Hellenistic world as the addressees of their poetry. In the Roman world the already existing relationship between poets and patrons was extended to include the most important family in the Empire. The fact that the first Princeps wrote epigrams in his spare time created a welcome environment for practitioners of the genre.[46] One of the major representatives of the genre in the Augustan age was Crinagoras from Mytilene on the island of Lesbos. He visited Rome on several occasions as an ambassador before he decided, presumably in 26 BCE, to stay as a permanent resident. Crinagoras was sufficiently close to Augustus to accompany him on his military campaigns.[47] He is the author of two epigrams on Marcellus, the son of Augustus' sister Octavia. The earliest epigram serves as a companion to a gift, a copy of Callimachus' *Hecale* (*AP* 9.545). The second epigram celebrates Marcellus' safe return from the war front in Spain in 25 BCE, followed by the shaving of his first beard (*AP* 6.161).[48]

After Marcellus' unexpected death in 23 BCE Crinagoras' imperial output continued. An epigram published around 20 BCE praises Tiberius for placing Tigranes on the throne of Armenia (*APl* 61). Next in the chronological sequence are three poems for a female member of the imperial family. Her identity is not entirely certain and it cannot even be established whether all three epigrams concern the same woman. If they do, however, and this seems very likely, it suggests that after Octavia, Crinagoras found another member of the family willing to support him financially. The most explicit epigram is a prayer directed at Hera asking her to facilitate the pregnancy of a woman by the name of Antonia (*AP* 6.244). Octavia had two daughters named Antonia, usually distinguished from one another by referring to them as Antonia Maior and Minor. Not much is known about the Elder Antonia and consequently most scholars agree that the epigram is addressed to the Younger Antonia, who was married to Drusus, the brother of Tiberius, and who was pregnant with her son Germanicus in 16 or 15 BCE.[49] Two other epigrams are addressed to an unidentified female member of the imperial family and on the basis of *AP* 6.244 it is assumed that the woman in these epigrams was also Antonia.[50] In the first of the two epigrams a gift of winter roses is made to a woman who is about to be married (*AP* 6.345). Antonia may have married Drusus in the early spring of 18 BCE.[51] A woman of the imperial family received five books of lyrical poetry, presumably as a birthday present (*AP* 9.239). There is no hard evidence that Crinagoras ever received financial support from Octavia and Antonia, or from Augustus for that matter, but the possibility is a strong one seeing the important moments concerning the imperial family covered in them.[52] It is therefore no surprise that he is traditionally catalogued as a court poet.[53] Crinagoras would have served as an obvious model for any poet with aspirations to be a successful writer of epigrams. His influence on Martial, either by way of his poetry or by his focus on the imperial family, is acknowledged, although it is left largely undefined.[54]

On the side of Greek epigram the biggest influence on Martial is Lucillius, a poet who was active in Rome under Nero and whose poems survive in the Palatine Anthology.[55] Martial incorporated two aspects of Lucillius' work that the latter had developed into important features of his poetry.[56] His major contribution is the development of the skoptic epigram, a type of epigram in which ridicule is heaped on physical defects, immoral excesses, and other types of unwanted social behavior. Also singled out for vilification were certain occupations that were deemed of questionable reputation, such as doctors, undertakers, and innkeepers, because of the nature of the work, their obsession with money or the perceived incompetence of the practitioners. These themes make up a substantial amount of Martial's poetry. The second area in which Lucillius' influence is undeniable is in the projection of the emperor as a reader of the poet's work. His importance becomes immediately clear when his imperial epigrams are compared to the way in which Lucillius' predecessor Crinagoras uses the emperor as subject material for his epigrams. Of Crinagoras only a single epigram (*AP* 9.562) is known in which the emperor is the subject matter and where he is addressed explicitly as Kaisar, the usual form of address for the emperor in the Greek world at the time.[57] Lucillius' relationship with his emperor is entirely different. He commandeers Nero as a reader (*AP* 11.75; 11.116; 11.132; 11.185; 11.247), even though the emperor is by no means connected with the subject matter of the poem.[58] In the poem that the epigrammatist explicitly claims is the proem to his second book of epigrams, Lucillius states in the final couplet that a few coppers (the epigram has *chalkos*; "bronze") from Nero have enabled him to survive as a poet (*AP* 9.572).[59] The issue as to whether Nero was a, or even the main, patron of Lucillius cannot be resolved without new evidence, but it is possible that Lucillius' emperor is an entirely literary construct.

Apart from Callimachus (4.23; 10.4), the names of the Greek epigrammatists discussed here are absent from Martial's epigrams.[60] The lack of any reference to Lucillius is especially revealing, because no fewer than seventeen of Martial's epigrams are based on the work of his predecessor.[61] The vast majority of these epigrams are much more than attempts at emulation; in some cases it is much better to speak of direct translations without modifications.[62] For a poet who is so concerned with defending his poetry against plagiarism and exposing impostors, it is ironic, to say the least, that he is happy to pass off as his own the poems of others.[63] The absence of references to Greek epigrammatists, either of earlier times or of Martial's own lifetime, is by design. It is Martial's desire to rewrite epigram as a Roman genre, which may also explain why he seeks to establish a literary connection between his own work and that of Catullus.[64] The debt is expressed most eloquently in 10.78, where Martial asks his friend Baebius Macer, who is on his way to take up the governorship of Dalmatia, not to prefer his predecessors over him but to rank him below Catullus only. In another poem from the same book, 10.103, Martial is less modest, stating that Verona, the birthplace of Catullus, would happily adopt him as her son if Bilbilis does not want him anymore.[65]

Other Roman predecessors of Martial include L. Cornelius Lentulus Gaetulicus, Albinovanus Pedo, and Domitius Marsus. All three are mentioned together with Catullus in Martial's prose preface of the first book of his epigrams. These poets are unknown to the modern reader and mere names to the regular Classicist. Due to the small number of lines that survive for each poet it is therefore difficult to say what kind of poetry they produced and how much of an influence they had on Martial. Domitius Marsus is known for two poems about Atia, the mother of Octavian, which have survived in a late anthology (*Epigrammata Bobiensia* 39; 40). Lentulus Gaetulicus is known for a flattering epigram addressed to Caligula, the same emperor, ironically, who had him executed in 39 CE for involvement in a conspiracy. In striking contrast with Martial, who specialized in epigram, his predecessors produced works in other genres as well. Albinovanus Pedo was the author of an epic poem on the Athenian hero Theseus (Ovid's *Epistulae ex Ponto* 4.10 is addressed to Albinovanus; Ovid's *Ars Amatoria* 2.24 is a line from the poem; *Amores* 2.11.10 is another one) and a historical epic on the campaigns of Germanicus (for a snippet, see Seneca the Elder, *Suasoriae* 1.15), while Domitius Marsus wrote a theoretical work on wit (Quintilian, *The Orator's Education* 6.3.102).

Until a few years ago the scholarly position on the date and nature of Martial's debut as a poet was firmly established. The *Liber Spectaculorum* ("The Book of the Games") was a collection of epigrams on highlights of gladiatorial games held by a Flavian emperor. The similarities with reports in Dio Cassius (*Roman History* 66.25) and Suetonius (*Life of Titus* 7.3) on the games celebrated by Titus during the opening of the Colosseum in 80 led to the conclusion that Martial's poems must have appeared in a single collection soon after the events they are describing. In the chronology of Martial's output this was his first published work. Recent research, however, has convincingly argued that some of the poems in the *Liber Spectaculorum* should be taken to refer to games organized by Domitian between 83 and 85.[66] This suggests that, while some of the poems could have been written as early as 80, the *Liber Spectaculorum* may have appeared as a collection as late as 85 or 86. The idea has already been met with support and seems poised to completely overtake the idea of a publication shortly after the opening of the Colosseum.[67] The order in which Martial's books of epigrams were published is now thought to be as follows. Two books of occasional poetry, the *Xenia* and the *Apophoreta*, were published in 83 (Leary, *Xenia* 13) and 84 or 85 (Leary, *Apophoreta* 10), respectively. After the *Liber Spectaculorum*, Martial published twelve books of epigrams between 86 and 101.[68]

Nero's suicide in June of 68 was followed by a disruptive and disastrous civil war. Three ambitious senators, Galba, Otho, and Vitellius, only managed to hold on to power for a short period of time before Vespasian, from a family—the Flavii—with roots in rural Umbria, successfully used his legions in Syria to take over absolute control over the Roman Empire and establish a new dynasty. Vespasian is best known for his efforts to bring economic rigor to the Roman Empire after years of extravagance under Nero (Suetonius, *Life of Vespasian* 23.3; Dio Cassius, *Roman History* 65.14.5; Juvenal, *Satires* 14.204–5) and for his lighthearted attitude on his deathbed toward his imminent deification (Suetonius, *Life of Vespasian* 23.4; Dio Cassius, *Roman History* 66.17.3).[69] The reign of his eldest son Titus (79–81) was marked by two major events: the destruction of Herculaneum, Pompeii, and Stabiae by the eruption of Mount Vesuvius in 79 (Dio Cassius, *Roman History* 21–23; Suetonius, *Life of Titus* 8.3–4) and the opening of the

Colosseum one year later (Dio Cassius, *Roman History* 66.25; Suetonius, *Life of Titus* 7.3). Titus suddenly died in the prime of his life in 81. Martial's productive and prolific years as a poet coincided with the ten years between 86 and 96, the year in which Titus' successor, his younger brother Domitian, was assassinated. In this period Martial wrote more than ninety epigrams addressed to Domitian, roughly ten percent of his total output until 96. The vast majority of them praise the emperor for his military successes and his social and moral legislation, usually in combination with an attempt to acquire his financial support. Martial does not seem to have been particularly successful in acquiring the patronage of the emperor and the material advantages that would accrue from such a relationship. That was certainly not for lack of trying. Especially books 5 and 8 feature a large number of poems dedicated to the emperor and the prose letter that serves as the dedication for book 8 is a dapper attempt to persuade Domitian to acknowledge and reward the poet's eloquent and elegant poetry.

The poems in praise of Domitian have been a controversial issue in the scholarship on Martial since the nineteenth century and although different viewpoints have been taken, the controversy is not yet resolved. In the nineteenth century and for most of the twentieth century Martial was viewed as a self-contradictory poet. He was praised for his sharp insights on the social lapses of his fellow Romans but criticized for the obscenity of his poetry as well as for his flattery of Domitian. J. H. Westcott called his flattery assiduous and importunate, marking out the persistent nature of his praise and the unwelcome response this created in the contemporary reader. Edwin Post called him a consummate lickspittle and a time-serving hypocrite.[70] Only occasionally is the criticism mitigated by a sense that Martial had very few options: "Apart from the grossness of some of his verses, the poet's chief weakness lay in the spirit of abject flattery that marks his allusions to Domitian. This, however, was the vice of the day, a fawning servility being the only road to favour with such a ruler, beneath whose sway any independence of character on the part of a man of note was likely to cost him his life."[71] The notion that Martial was a servile poet has not completely died out. A history of Roman literature published toward the close of the twentieth century labels Martial's eulogies of Domitian as "disgusting."[72]

In the final quarter of the twentieth century scholars developed a different approach to Martial's adulation; disgust with Martial's sycophancy made way for admiration for his ingenuity.[73] Point of departure is the notion that Martial took great care in putting together each book of epigrams from a "back catalog" of poems that had been circulating informally among buyers and addressees. The poems that praise Domitian are then studied together with those poems that stand in closest proximity to them on the assumption that the adulation is somehow undone or subverted by additional meaning flowing over from the other poems. This reading strategy became very influential in the scholarship on Martial in the final two decades of the twentieth century, but toward the close of the century more and more scholars started to question the premises underlying this literary strategy. One of the convincing objections maintains that Domitian was well-educated, smart, and well-versed in the reading of literature. To assume, therefore, that he was incapable of spotting the hidden meanings embedded by Martial in the structure of his books seems, in hindsight, to be somewhat naïve.[74]

What is perhaps most striking in this shift in perspective on the relationship between Martial and Domitian is the fact that Domitian's image as a cruel despot has been left virtually unaltered. The image of Domitian as a cruel emperor is based on a variety of hostile accounts (Tacitus' biography of his father-in-law, Agricola; Suetonius' biography of Domitian; Pliny the Younger's *Panegyricus* in praise of Trajan; Juvenal's fourth satire). These accounts were without exception composed after the death of the emperor and although they are interesting for the

composite picture they provide of Domitian's personality, they
do not present a reliable basis for evaluating his reign. Ancient
historians have paid very little attention to the historical puzzle
that is Domitian and when they have, they have analyzed him
almost exclusively without the help of Martial's epigrams.[75] In
the past twenty-five years Domitian has received more atten-
tion because of the rise in interest in Martial, Statius, and most
recently Pliny, but for this purpose the rhetorical image of Do-
mitian does not need to be corrected. Martial's "Domitian" is
worthy of consideration because it shows that there also existed
positive accounts of the emperor. It is good to suspend judg-
ment and to examine which aspects of Domitian received the
attention of the poet.

     In ancient Rome, imperial building projects did not only
offer the city population an important opportunity to earn a
living, but each completed assignment potentially carried a
multitude of cultural and political messages. Domitian ranks
second only behind Augustus as an initiator of large building
projects. Domitian was responsible for the rebuilding and res-
toration of many temples damaged in the fire of 64.[76] In 28 BCE
Augustus had undertaken the restoration of eighty-two temples
that had fallen into disrepair (Augustus, *Res Gestae* 20). By imi-
tating this Domitian exemplified his overall religious zeal and
devotion to the gods. He also commissioned the building of
new temples dedicated to his patron goddess Minerva (in the
forum), and to Castor and Pollux, Isis and Serapis. His other
main line of building activities consisted of projects to add luster
to the Flavian family, the first set of emperors not connected
with Augustus, the founder of the Principate. Their most famous
building project, the massive amphitheater officially named the
Amphitheatrum Flavium or Flavianum but better known as
the Colosseum, blotted out the reputation of Nero, who had
built a park connected with his Golden House on the same
location. Domitian further promoted the illustrious reputation
of the Flavian family by building a sumptuously decorated

structure that was monument and temple in one on the site of his father's house on the Quirinal Hill. The building was given a presumptuous name—*templum gentis Flaviae*, the sanctuary of the Flavian gens—another reason perhaps for the ill will sensed by some groups in Roman society. It plays an important role in Martial's imperial panegyrics of book 9 (9.1; 9.3.12; 9.20.1; 9.34.2; 9.93.6).[77] The poet is equally enthusiastic about the imperial palace that Domitian commissioned on the Palatine (7.56; 8.36; 9.24). Another building that attracted the attention of the poet was a dining hall nicknamed "the Golden Crumb" (*mica aurea*; 2.59 [page 19]).[78]

Domitian was the first Roman emperor who allegedly insisted that he should be addressed as Lord and God (*dominus et deus*), which ancient authors and modern scholars identify as an important reason for his growing unpopularity in the final years of his reign.[79] In his *Life of Domitian*, Suetonius (13.1–2) lists a number of incidents illustrating the emperor's arrogance and here we find the evidence for his alleged belief in his divinity. On one occasion the emperor was delighted to hear the crowd in the Colosseum greet him and his wife as Lord and Lady (*domino et dominae*). He further points to a letter that the emperor sent to his procurators insisting that he be addressed (in writing) as Lord and God. Suetonius stresses that this then became the customary address of the emperor, both in writing and in conversation (13.2). Suetonius' reference to this instruction cannot be dated, but in his discussion of the same events the historian Dio Cassius (67.4.7) places it very close to the death of Cornelius Fuscus, whose armies were routed by the Dacians in 86. Procurators were middle-level administrators of equestrian rank who directly served the emperor, and it is perhaps unnecessary to assume that what was applied to these officials was imposed on all subjects of the Roman Empire. The tradition that Domitian insisted on being worshipped as a god is late and influenced by strong anti-Domitianic sentiments. The first poem by Martial in which Domitian is addressed as

Lord and God was published as part of book 5 (5.8.1). The most likely date of publication of this book of epigrams is toward the end of the year 90. Other poems in which Martial uses this form of address are 7.34.8–9, 8.2.6, and 9.66.3 (page 74). In an epigram published after Domitian's assassination (10.72), Martial finally distances himself from his obsequiousness. The poem is addressed to a group of "Flatteries" that have come to visit the poet to be used in another epigram, but Martial states that there is no place for them in Rome anymore and sends them to the Parthian Empire.[80] In the end Martial's apology for his obsequiousness also serves to promote the idea that praise for Domitian's successor took place in an environment that is sincere.

Throughout Domitian's reign his relationship with the Senate was difficult, but it is generally agreed that the relationship was at its lowest ebb during the final part of his rule. It used to be convention to refer to the period from 93 onward as a reign of terror, but more recently scholars have suggested dates earlier in the reign as the start of more serious conflict.[81] Domitian's rule ended on 18 September 96 when the emperor succumbed to a palace conspiracy. The Greek historian Dio Cassius and the Roman biographer Suetonius provide a list of conspirators and a number of reasons that encouraged them to act. There are slight discrepancies between the two lists, but in essence the two can be said to agree on the fact that Domitian was murdered by freedmen in the imperial administration, perhaps with the tacit support of the emperor's wife, Domitia Longina (Dio Cassius, *Roman History* 67.15.2; Suetonius, *Life of Domitian* 14.1).[82] The main conspirators are identified as Parthenius, Domitian's chamberlain and the addressee of a number of Martial's epigrams, and Stephanus, the freedman and accountant of Domitian's niece Domitilla (Suetonius, *Life of Domitian* 14.1; Dio Cassius, *Roman History* 67.15.1). They decided to kill Domitian because of his growing arrogance and for the execution of two courtiers, Epaphroditus (Suetonius, *Life of Domitian* 14.4; allegedly on the grounds that he was thought to have assisted in the killing of Nero, close to thirty years before) and Domitian's cousin Flavius Clemens (15.1; on a slight suspicion). At an arranged meeting Stephanus stabbed the emperor in the groin, after which additional muscle was provided by three low-ranking palace officials and a gladiator from the imperial school (Suetonius, *Life of Domitian* 17.1). After his death the senate met to condemn Domitian's memory by having his name erased from all public inscriptions and to have his sculpture and portraits defaced (Suetonius, *Life of Domitian* 23.1; Pliny the Younger, *Panegyricus* 52). If we may believe Suetonius, the senators had ladders brought into the meeting hall to take down the emperor's portraits and the shields inscribed with his virtues and applauded the spectacle of seeing them being smashed to pieces on the floor (23.1). This was the second occasion, after Nero, on which an emperor suffered the systematic erasing of his existence, a process known as *damnatio memoriae*.[83] The consequences for Martial cannot be spelled out in detail, but the joyful reaction to the toppling of Domitian by the senators suggests that literary patrons may no longer have been forthcoming for one who over the years had lent his voice to the emperor's policies and had consistently praised his military successes.

Martial published book 10 at the beginning of 96 but decided to withdraw it, presumably immediately after Domitian's assassination, and published book 11 in December of 96 (Sullivan, *Martial* 46). Book 10 was reissued in a second version in 98 (see discussion above). This means that from the start of Nerva's reign in September of 96 Martial made two attempts to adjust to the new political climate, the one premeditated, the other one imposed or self-imposed. The process of withdrawing a book from circulation and replacing it with a less offensive edition must have been a humiliating experience for the poet. He decided to return to Bilbilis. There are two schools of thought on this issue. One is represented by Howell ("Martial's Return") and believes that dissatisfaction with the life of a client in Rome (see 10.70 and 10.74 [page 84]) was the reason for his retirement. The other one is supported by Sullivan (*Martial* 47) and argues that Martial could not make the transition to the new set of emperors. The second option seems to have the most supporters.[84]

An event taking place close to one year after Domitian's assassination may have had a big impact on Martial's confidence that his career could survive the political turmoil. In 97 the Praetorian Guard was successful in demanding the execution of Parthenius, one of the conspirators against Domitian.[85] In December of 96, four months after Domitian's assassination, Martial had addressed the opening poem of book 11 to Parthenius. At the time of its publication Parthenius had not yet been removed from the imperial household, although it is hard to imagine that he was allowed to continue under Nerva in his position as *cubicularius*.[86] His execution removed more than an old patron from Martial's circle; it ended the hope of a successful continuation of his career in Rome.[87]

Another way to show that Martial's discomfort with Rome after 96 was inspired by the political situation is by examining the epigrams addressed to the new emperors Nerva and Trajan. There is no evidence that he was more successful in acquiring the financial support of Nerva and Trajan than he was with Domitian. His persistent attempts to establish a rapport with Domitian's successors demonstrate to what degree Martial had become accustomed to define his position as a writer within the political environment of Rome. His positive evaluation of his chances to connect with Nerva was aided perhaps by the fact that he had already addressed two epigrams to him before he became emperor and the fact that Nerva was a poet himself (8.70; 9.26). In the first epigram addressed to Nerva as emperor (11.2), Martial immediately defines his reign as one in which the spirit of the Saturnalia—with the emphasis on ordered license—is celebrated, intimating (hoping is a better word) that his poetry would be greeted more favorably by the present emperor than by his predecessor. Three other epigrams identify Nerva by name (11.4; 11.7; 12.5),[88] while there are four epigrams addressed to Trajan (10.6, where he is described as "leader"; 10.7; 10.34; 12.8).[89] Studies of the poems addressed to Nerva and Trajan generally conclude that these are less committed and less effective than the epigrams he wrote for Domitian. It seems not unjustified to conclude that Martial was unable to make the transition to the new political reality of the post-Domitianic period. Sullivan (*Martial* 51) rightly emphasizes that Trajan was a military man with very little interest in literature. Martial decided to leave Rome for good and returned to Bilbilis. This is reflected in two epigrams that are significantly placed at the very end of book 10 (10.103; 10.104).

In 10.103 the matter of Martial's return has not yet been resolved. Indeed, he threatens to turn around if Bilbilis does not want him back. In between the writing of 103 and 104 Martial must have received some positive feedback because in 104 he sends his tenth book to Bilbilis together with Flavus before embarking on the journey himself. The personified book is instructed to greet some longstanding friends and to find its "parent" (*parentem*) a pleasant accommodation at a reasonable price. For Martial, the sending of a book to Bilbilis was an extraordinary reversal from his earlier practice of sending books of epigrams to patrons in Rome or up the Palatine in the hope of acquiring financial support from the imperial administration. The scenario of 104 suggests that Martial returned to Spain after the publication of his revised tenth book.[90] The return is anticipated in a number of epigrams, starting with 10.13, addressed to one Manius, and continuing with 10.92, where Martial commends his piece of land in Nomentum to its new owner, Marrius from Atina. The book is usually thought to have been published around the middle of 98. Possibly the latest datable epigram in the book is the birthday epigram in honor of Claudius Restitutus, which is set around the Kalends of October, but may of course have been written in anticipation of the actual event. Publication of the book, therefore, must be situated at the latest in September. It is unlikely, although not impossible, that Martial sailed to Spain in winter when regular shipping was discontinued; it makes more sense to assume that he left in the late spring or early summer of the next year.

Once reestablished in Bilbilis, Martial produced a final book of epigrams, which he sent from Spain to Rome, perhaps in 101 or 102 (Sullivan, *Martial* 52). Upon his return Martial received a plot of land from a woman called Marcella (12.21; 12.31 [page 100]). She is obviously someone of high social standing, for Martial addresses her as *domina* (12.31.7), a term that is also used for Violentilla (6.21.3), the wife of Martial's patron Arruntius Stella.[91] Her evident importance to the poet's life in Bilbilis did not result in the dedication of the book to her. This honor is reserved for Terentius Priscus (12 *epist.*; 12.1; 12.3; 12.62), who is explicitly identified as the poet's Maecenas (12.3.1–4), although it is unclear what Terentius did to earn this accolade.[92] Despite the fact that the book was written in Spain, the number of epigrams devoted to Martial's Spain is not excessively high. The book might as well have been conceived and written in Rome. Even though he is no longer in Rome, Martial seeks out high-ranking Romans, such as Istantius Rufus who became governor of Baetica at the beginning of the second century CE (12.98). The two had already been in contact in Rome (7.68; 8.50.21; 8.73). Like most of Martial's friends, he was a writer himself and had a certain interest in scabrous poetry. Apart from the epigrams addressed to Trajan, there are other epigrams that cultivate a relationship with an individual in Rome: 12.2 (addressed to his patron L. Arruntius Stella); 12.34 (to his longtime friend Julius Martialis [page 101]). The most famous epigram in this book is addressed to the satirist Juvenal (12.18 [page 99]) and makes the most of the contrast between sweaty, noisy, busy Rome and idle, relaxed, lazy Bilbilis.

In a letter (*Ep.* 3.21) dated to 104 CE the Roman senator Pliny the Younger reports to his friend Cornelius Priscus that the poet Martial had passed away. Pliny's comments read as a ringing endorsement of Martial's serious commitment to literature. His well-earned reputation as a poet is only undone by the low status of epigram in the Roman world. In other words, Martial was a talented poet, but in the eyes of some he did not qualify as a great one because the genre in which he decided to write was ranked very low in terms of literary respectability. Pliny and his correspondent agree that Martial's epigrams will not survive his death for very long. Since Pliny was not in the habit of expressing a judgment that was destined to go against the opinions of other members of his class, it must be assumed that his assessment of Martial's epigrams was shared by many (other) members of the sophisticated elite. Notwithstanding this, modern critics triumphantly point out that Pliny was hopelessly wrong in his assessment of the chances for survival of Martial's work.[93] Pliny reveals that Martial made the return journey to Spain thanks to a subvention that he provided in gratitude for an epigram by the poet, something that is not recorded by the poet. For the contents of the epigram he refers Cornelius Priscus to Martial's published work, but it just happens that he knows some of the lines by heart. He summarizes the first eleven lines and quotes the final ten lines of the epigram in full. The letter is the only external source of information on the poet; as such it is ideally placed to produce a perspective on Martial and his poetry that is based on a reader's response, not on the signposts left behind by the poet.

Martial's epigram (10.20) is framed as a road map for Thalia, the Muse of Epigram, to make the trip from the poet's house on the Quirinal to Pliny's residence on the Esquiline (*Ep.* 3.21.5).[94] Once Thalia has arrived at her destination she is given further details about how to approach Pliny: with circumspection. The man is a workaholic who spends all his time writing speeches for delivery in the centumviral court, speeches that future generations will compare to those of Cicero. Because of his commitment to his work he should only be visited when the hour is late (implying that he is unavailable for the morning *salutatio*), when Lyaeus (the "deliverer of cares"; another name for the god Bacchus) runs wild and people let their hair hang down. In the evening even stiff Catos read Martial's poetry. Cato the Younger, who committed suicide rather than receive Julius Caesar's pardon, serves as the proverbial blocking reader in Martial's poetry (1 *epist.*; 1.8; 9.28; 11.2; 11.15; 11.39; 12.3). He is a spoilsport who needs to be removed from the book and from the theater that he inadvertently enters (1 *epist.* 18, where the theater stands for Martial's book of epigrams).[95] The epigram addressed to Pliny the Younger is the only poem in Martial's collection in which Cato is represented as a reader of epigrams. I cannot escape the feeling that Martial's epigram is written in jest as a comical exaggeration of Pliny's character. If Martial's epigram was a mixture of praise and (light) jest, Pliny's text is perhaps a layered response to this.[96]

Pliny's description of Martial's personality and poetry is commonly translated in glowing terms, as the following example demonstrates: "he was a man of great gifts, with a mind both subtle and penetrating, and his writings are remarkable for their combination of sincerity with pungency and wit."[97] The words selected to describe Martial (*ingeniosus*; *acutus*; *acer*) are the very same ones with which Cicero characterizes ne'er do wells and other annoying opponents (*ingeniosissimus* in *pro Murena* 48 and *acutissimus* in *pro Cluentio* 67). Moreover, *ingeniosus* denotes the irritatingly clever speaker rather than the man of subtle brilliance, while *acutus* suggests a scheming individual. *Acer*, finally, denotes keen ruthlessness. In conclusion, "By calling Martial *homo ingeniosus*, *acutus*, *acer*, Pliny has strung the poet up with the noose of that *ingeniosissimus* orator, M. Tullius Cicero."[98] The use of Ciceronian rhetorical terms is made more compelling by the fact that Martial compares Pliny's qualities as an orator with those of Cicero. It can further be shown that Pliny's words present a sequence of increasingly negative sentiments, even though the second string of labels is presented in a different order, with the least hostile sentiment (*candor*) standing in last place (although modified by "no less"). The climactic labels in each sequence are the adjective *acer* ("sharp"; "stinging") and the noun *fel* ("bitter gall," and hence "hatefulness"; "poison"). Both *fel* and *acer* are used by Martial to characterize his poetry (but not his personality). Epigram 7.25 (page 58) is a defense of his version of epigram against a rival whose poetry is described as squeaky clean and syrupy. Martial's poetry is characterized by a high level of acidity, with copious amounts of salt, bitter gall, and vinegar (*acetum*). Pliny's obituary of Martial could then also be translated as: "he was a smart-ass, a schemer, and a bitterly cruel man. In his writing he injected a lack of respect and hatefulness, all wrapped in frankness." It is an appropriate response to an epigram (10.20) that comically misrepresents Pliny on essential points, and it is a tribute of which Martial would have been proud.

## Abbreviations

AE *L'Année épigraphique*; annual publication of the Centre national de la recherche scientifique (CNRS) in Paris. Each volume presents newly discovered and revised Latin inscriptions published in scholarly books, museum collections, and journals for a particular year.

AP *Anthologia Palatina*; collection of Greek poems and epigrams discovered in 1606 in the Palatine library in Heidelberg, Germany.

APl *Anthologia Planudea*; collection of Greek epigrams made by the Byzantine scholar Maximus Planudes in the thirteenth century.

CIL *Corpus Inscriptionum Latinarum*; founded in 1853 in Berlin by Theodor Mommsen and still in progress; collection of Latin inscriptions in seventeen volumes; each volume is divided in subvolumes; the allocation of inscriptions to each volume is made on the basis of geographical origin, with the exception of volumes 1 (the oldest Roman inscriptions until the death of Julius Caesar), 15 (*instrumentum domesticum*; inscriptions on objects for daily use and domestic utensils); 16 (military diplomas); and 17 (milestones).

## Notes

1. For a useful discussion in English of the development of the site and its public buildings, see Mierse 149–73. For the suggestion that the temple was dedicated to the imperial cult, see Mierse 159. The site has been excavated by Manuel Martín-Bueno and a large group of collaborators from the University of Zaragoza. Their findings have been published in numerous articles and chapters in books, all of them in Spanish.

2. See Curchin 82.

3. See Noy.

4. In his attacks on undesirable social and moral behavior Martial claims to focus on vices rather than on individuals (10.33.9–10), suggesting that the latter, even though they appear in a world that seems to be Rome, only exist to convey the vices of the time.

5. It is interesting that this comment appears in an epigram addressed to the emperor Domitian. It deliberately complicates a reading of Martial's poetry.

6. With the significant exception of the poems in the *Liber Spectaculorum* ("The Book of the Games"); see Coleman, *M. Valerii Martialis Liber Spectaculorum* lxxxi–lxxxii. A different kind of exception is provided by 1.5, where the speaker is Domitian, an experiment that is not repeated.

7. These are generally accepted to be Martial's parents, despite an attempt by Mantke to make them the parents of Martial's dead slave Erotion. As Howell (*Martial: Epigrams V* 117) has demonstrated, this low social status is incompatible with the highly formal label *patronos* of 5.34.7.

8. The fact that the poet calls his parents *stulti* (lit. "stupid") should be read in an ironic way ("simplistic" or "simple-minded"). The virtuous principle of a good education is worthless in contemporary Rome where money decides everything.

9. Bridge and Lake vii; Post xi; Sullivan, *Martial* 2; Henriksén 90. Inscriptions from Hispania Tarraconensis provide evidence for the existence of teachers of grammar and literature: *CIL* 2.7.336 (Cordoba; the only *grammaticus Graecus* thus far attested in Spain); *CIL* 2.14.377 (Saguntum); *CIL* 2.2892 (Tritium Megallum); *CIL* 2.5079 (Astorga); *CIL* 2.14.3.1282 (Tarraco); *CIL* 2.2892 (a *grammaticus Latinus* from Clunia who taught in Tarraco; see Fear). Teachers of rhetoric have been attested in Gades (*CIL* 2.1738; Cadiz), Tarraco, and Collippo; see Keay 86. Tarraco was also the city where the emperor

Augustus heard Gavius Silo declaim in 26–25 BCE (Seneca the Elder, *Controversiae* 10 pref. 14).

10.  Pliny the Younger (*Letters* 2.14.10) quotes Quintilian: *adsectabar Domitium Afrum* ("I attached myself to Domitius Afer"); cf. Quintilian, *The Orator's Education* 5.7.7: *Domitio Afro . . . quem adulescentulus senem colui* ("Domitius Afer with whom I trained when he was an old man and I was an adolescent"). Quintilian (*The Orator's Education* 10.1.118) praises Domitius Afer. The verb *assector* is the correct technical term for a kind of internship with a trained orator; Tacitus (*A Dialogue on Oratory* 2.1) had attached himself as a young man to Marcus Aper and Julius Secundus.

11.  Sullivan, "Was Martial Really Married?"; Sullivan, *Martial* 25–26; Williams 280; Howell, *Martial* 16.

12.  Bell (22) argues for multiple marriages and at least one daughter, possibly Erotion. Ascher points out that, with the exception of the grant of the *ius trium liberorum*, it is virtually impossible to derive any information on Martial's domestic life from his poetry. See Sullivan's reply to Ascher's article: Sullivan, "Was Martial Really Married?"

13.  Martial refers to this privilege in a series of epigrams: 2.91; 2.92 [page 22]; 3.95; 9.97.

14.  Pliny the Younger (*Letters* 10.94.2) requested the privilege for his friend the biographer Suetonius who was married but had not produced any offspring. Watson and Watson (3) read *quod Fortuna vetat* ("what Fortune has denied me") in 2.91.5 as a reference to an infertile marriage. However, in 2.92.2 (page 22) the poet argues that he received the privilege for his literary output.

15.  Sullivan (*Martial* 44) suggests that it was published in mid-98, but it is not clarified on what basis this can be established.

16.  For the date of publication of the original book, see Fearnley 617. Watson and Watson (1n2) assume that the original book 10 was published in 95.

17.  Most scholars argue that Martial's year of birth fell between 38 and 41; cf. Watson and Watson 1, 1n2; Williams 4. Sullivan (*Martial* 2) departs from the same point of view but admits that 41 is more likely than any of the other years. Howell (*Martial* 9) opts for 40.

18.  In other poems (9.52 [page 73]; 12.60) Martial also makes his birthday the topic of his poetry, but he only indicates his age in 10.24.

19.  For Otho's suicide, see Edwards 35–39.

20.  They are briefly mentioned together in an epigram that celebrates

Domitian's victory over the Chatti (2.2). The objective of the epigram is to praise Domitian for single-handedly achieving military glory, whereas the triumph over the Jews had to be shared between Vespasian and Titus. Vespasian is mentioned alone, but not by name, in an epigram highlighting the monument and temple dedicated to the Flavian family (9.34). Titus is only mentioned by name in connection with his baths on the Esquiline Hill (3.20.15; 3.36.6).

21. See Watson and Watson 2: "honing his skills as an epigrammatist."

22. On two occasions Sullivan calls a Spaniard in Rome "one of Martial's many Spanish connections": *Martial* 16 (on Decianus); 19 (on Valerius Licinianus).

23. For the reasons of the ban, see Gresseth; Ahl; Griffin (278) places the ban around mid-64.

24. Griffin (148) and Sullivan (*Martial* 3) explicitly accept that all four named individuals were from the reign of Nero. Piso should then be identified as Caius Calpurnius Piso, the leader of the anti-Neronian conspiracy of 65; Memmius as Caius Memmius Regulus (Sullivan mistakenly has Gemellus), the consul of 63; Crispus as Q. Vibius Crispus, the suffect consul of 61. The last two individuals have no reputation as patrons of the arts and it is therefore more plausible that Memmius should be identified as Caius Memmius, the patron of Lucretius. If this is correct, the theory of four patrons from the reign of Nero is already seriously weakened.

25. For a detailed discussion of the relationship between Martial and Seneca, see Kleijwegt. For a restatement of the argument that Seneca was Martial's patron, see Nauta 52, 86–87.

26. This is the main point for Nauta to argue that Lucan may have been Martial's patron; see Nauta 87.

27. The first three books of the *Silvae* were published as a set in the early part of 93; see Newlands 3.

28. The suggestion that the poems were intended to celebrate the fiftieth anniversary of Lucan's birthday was made by Buchheit, "Statius' Geburtstagsgedicht zu Ehren Lucans" 231n3. See also Buchheit, "Martials Beitrag zum Geburtstag Lucans als Zyklus." For the date of publication of book 7 (December 92), see Sullivan, *Martial* 39; cf. 7.8. This does not mean that the poems were not written for the occasion in 89.

29. It is therefore imperative to examine in more detail Martial's conceptualization of literary patronage and to adopt a fresh perspective on this issue. One of the options that needs to be considered is that the epigrams do

not automatically present a comprehensive narrative of Martial's patronal relationships. It is possible that Martial regarded someone as his patron after one successful commission.

30. Sullivan (*Martial* 317) has the relationship start in 64.

31. The addressee of 4.55 is one Lucius who is traditionally identified by many scholars as Lucius Valerius Licinianus because he features in two other poems on Bilbilis.

32. For a detailed discussion of the identification, see Howell, *Commentary* 213–14. Howell eventually concludes that the two are one and the same person. The condemnation of the Vestal Virgin Cornelia and the exile of Licinianus took place in the period between 89 and 91. The Licinianus of 1.49, published in 86, appears to return to Spain permanently, which seems in conflict with the other information listed here. Howell (*Commentary* 214) suggests that the planned retirement was not carried through or that he changed his mind after having returned.

33. While in exile Licinianus taught rhetoric on Sicily (Pliny the Younger, *Letters* 4.11.1–4).

34. It has been suggested that he is identical with Marcus Cornelius Nigrinus Curiatius Maternus, though this individual is not from Bilbilis but originates from Liria near Valencia (*AE* 1973.383).

35. The name Maternus also appears as a respondent in two satirical epigrams, 1.96 and 2.74. No certainty can be had that all three poems refer to one and the same person. Howell (*Commentary* 306) has no doubts that they do, while Williams (234) is more cautious.

36. Albrecht 1039, where he appears in a list of sponsors of Martial's work; Stadter 8; Watson and Watson 90, where he is listed as a patron featured in 1.49 and 7.47.

37. It is argued by some (Nauta 62n70; Watson and Watson 90–91) that his first consulate was held in 86 or earlier, which suggests that he may have been politically active under Domitian. The argument in favor of a first consulate in 86 was made by Barnes but was refuted by Syme (272).

38. This is the conclusion drawn by Sullivan (*Martial* 19).

39. Williams 19.

40. Watson and Watson 2: "In all likelihood he circulated individual poems and small collections privately among potential patrons over a number of years, including them in the first two books of epigrams when these were published in 86–7."

41. Howell, *Commentary* 5.

42. Howell, *Commentary* 316.

43. Most scholars assume that Martial entered Rome as a poet looking for a network of patrons to sell his poetry. Sullivan (*Martial* 4) argues that by the time he produced the epigrams on the opening of the Colosseum, i.e. 80, he must already have had a considerable backlog of epigrams.

44. For Philodemus' epigrams, see Sider. Antipater of Thessalonica is the author of more than one hundred epigrams in the Greek Anthology, one of which (*AP* 7.626) was addressed to one of the grandsons of Augustus, either Lucius or Gaius; see Gow and Page, *The Garland of Philip* 2:419.

45. The Villa of the Papyri has revealed a large number of papyri scrolls, among which were found previously unknown works by Philodemus of Gadara. The architecture of the John Paul Getty Museum is based on the villa.

46. See Macrobius, *Saturnalia* 2.4.31, for an exchange between Augustus and an epigrammatist that leads to the payment of a monetary reward for an epigram (in this case by the epigrammatist for an epigram composed by the emperor); cf. Fitzgerald 29–30.

47. See Bowersock 36–37, who refers to *AP* 9.224 (a poem on a goat that traveled with the emperor because he liked goat's milk so much); *AP* 9.419 (an epigram on the healing springs of Dax in southwest France, presumably in connection with a serious illness that forced Augustus to withdraw from the Cantabrian War in 25 BCE; cf. Suetonius, *Life of the Deified Augustus* 81.1).

48. For the chronology of the epigrams, see Gow and Page, *The Garland of Philip* 2:212.

49. For the identification of the recipient of the gift as Antonia, see Gow and Page, *The Garland of Philip* 2:217; Hemelrijk 103–4.

50. Cameron chooses the Elder Julia, Augustus' daughter, as the addressee of *AP* 6.345.

51. See Kokkinos 11.

52. Sullivan (*Martial* 84) and Fitzgerald (29) call him a client of Octavia.

53. For instance by Syme (346), but the idea itself is much older; see Bowersock 36: "The household of Augustus could boast its own Greek poet to provide occasional verse."

54. Sullivan (*Martial* 85) suggests that Crinagoras should be identified as a court poet and that he "might well be taken as a model." This is also the viewpoint of Gow and Page, *The Garland of Philip* 2:239.

55. It is unknown whether he originated from the Greek speaking part of the Roman Empire or whether he was an educated Roman who wrote poetry in Greek. For an English translation of Lucillius' epigrams, see

Nystrom. For the influence of Greek epigram on Martial's poetry, see Neger, "*'Graece numquid' ait 'poeta nescis?'*"

56. The idea that Lucillius was a direct influence on Martial has been developed in detail by Holzberg (100–109).

57. The subject of the poem is a parrot that has escaped from its cage and continued to practice what it had been taught in the imperial palace: to say Hail Caesar. Inadvertently, all the other birds learn the same greeting from the parrot and are ready to pay obeisance to the emperor without being instructed to do so.

58. For the relationship between Lucillius and Nero, see Nisbet 113–34.

59. For a discussion of this poem, see Nisbet 37–47. Of course, the image of Nero that Lucillius has produced is that of a cheapskate; see Nisbet 40.

60. This is noted and commented upon by many scholars, among them Albrecht 2:1042. For Callimachus' influence on Martial, see Cowan.

61. Holzberg 29–30.

62. Livingstone and Nisbet (105–6) call Martial's epigram 6.12 (page 49) "a blatant reworking of a Lucillian original"; the original is *AP* 11.68. Scholarship on Martial has been more charitable toward the Spanish epigrammatist by using terms such as similarities and parallels; see Sullivan (*Martial* 88n50), who calls them "adaptations."

63. For Martial's response to poets who plagiarized his poetry, see Seo; McGill 74–113.

64. Fitzgerald (29) suggests that Domitian may have encouraged Roman poets to make inroads into genres traditionally dominated by Greek poets. If that were the case, we should expect a different response attributed to the emperor in Martial's epigrams.

65. For Martial's literary debt to Catullus, see Swann, *Martial's Catullus*; Swann, "*Sic scribit Catullus*"; Lorenz, "Catullus and Martial."

66. Holzberg (40) and Lorenz (*Erotik und Panegyrik* 57–59) already questioned whether the poems in the collection were connected with the opening of the Colosseum. More extensive research was undertaken by Coleman (*M. Valerii Martialis Liber Spectaculorum* li–lxv) and Buttrey, with the latter providing the key argument based on Domitian's coinage. One of the key items for associating some of the poems with Domitian is the rhinoceros featured in poems 9 and 26 of the *Liber Spectaculorum*. A rhinoceros appears on coins issued by Domitian between 83 and 85, and it seems very unlikely that he would do this after his brother had shown a similar animal during the opening of the Colosseum.

67. See Howell, *Martial* 15. Some do so with some degree of hesitation; see Neger, *Martials Dichtergedichte* 74.

68. Sullivan (*Martial* 52) argues that book 12 was put together toward December of 101.

69. Levick (101–13) does her best to show that the image of Vespasian as a parsimonious emperor is incorrect.

70. The most acidic and hilarious characterization of Martial as a sycophant was done by J. W. Mackail (194; quoted in Howell, *Martial* 63): "His perpetual flattery of Domitian, though gross as a mountain—it generally takes the form of comparing him with the Supreme Being, to the disadvantage of the latter."

71. Webb xv. Sullivan (*Martial* 76) is quite right in arguing that Martial's adulation of Domitian never seemed to be a problem for his later admirers who were accustomed to similar autocratic conditions.

72. Albrecht 2:1050.

73. See Garthwaite, "Domitian"; "Panegyrics"; "Patronage"; "Putting a Price"; "*Ludimus innocui.*" For a sociological reading of Martial's flattery, see Spisak 53–72.

74. Henriksén 16–21; Coleman, "Martial Book 8."

75. In English there are only two biographies of the emperor: Jones and Southern.

76. The Greek historian Dio Cassius (*Roman History* 66.24.2) has a list of all the buildings that were destroyed or damaged by the fire of 64, most of which were repaired by Domitian, as is proven by archaeological excavations.

77. For a discussion of the symbolical importance of this building, see Davies 148–58.

78. Its exact location has not been established; for discussion of the problems that make it difficult to identify its location, see Jones 86; Southern 128; Williams 199–200.

79. Southern 36, 45; cf. Jones (107–8), who argues that "whilst he did not ask or demand to be addressed as one (a god), he did not actively discourage the few flatterers who did."

80. Sullivan (*Martial* 76–77) highlights that Martial's apology, if that is what it is, is moving and unique in Roman literature.

81. Jones (77) points out that confiscations of property of opponents already started in 85, while Southern (114) views the year 89 as the starting point for more open conflict between emperor and Senate.

82. For an analysis of the conspiracy, see Jones 193–96; Southern 117–18; Grainger 4–28; Collins.

83. For the visual and artistic evidence of *damnatio memoriae*, see the discussion by Varner; for a discussion of the historical relevance of the process, see Flower.

84. Watson and Watson (4–5) give a fair summary of Martial's dissatisfaction with urban life, but they obviously find the political situation a much more compelling argument.

85. Dio Cassius (*Roman History* 68.3.3) mentions the execution of certain people at the insistence of the Praetorian Guard, but no names are mentioned and no connection with the assassination of Domitian is pointed out. One of the other people handed over for execution by Nerva was Petronius Secundus, a former prefect of the Guard; see Grainger 95. The execution of Parthenius is graphically described in the *Epitome de Caesaribus* 12.8, a work of dubious accuracy from the fourth century.

86. I therefore disagree with Sullivan, who argues (*Martial* 46) that Parthenius remained an influential figure during Nerva's reign because the new emperor must have felt indebted to his services. It is always dangerous to keep the murderers of your predecessor in the same position.

87. Kay (53) calls the address of the opening poem of book 11 to Parthenius "a political act, a sign of his allegiance to the new regime." This view is endorsed by Henriksén 15. Parthenius makes his final appearance in book 12 (12.11), which was published in 101, four years after the death of its subject, but it is suggested by Nauta (438n195) that 12.11 may have been inserted into book 12 by someone other than Martial.

88. It seems logical to add 10.72 to this list, even though Shackleton Bailey in his Loeb edition prefers to attribute this to Trajan, presumably because the emperor, who is never named directly by Martial, is described as *imperator*, which suggests a man with a military background, which Nerva was not. Epigrams 11.5 and 12.11.6 are addressed to Caesar and *dux* ("leader"), respectively, and should also be attributed to Nerva.

89. It is perhaps significant that in book 10 there is no epigram addressed to Nerva.

90. For the date of Martial's return, see Howell, "Martial's Return" 173; Watson and Watson 3. Henderson (83n5) suggests 100.

91. Martial otherwise reserves the term for the city of Rome; see 1.3.3; 9.64.4. In 12.21 Martial pays Marcella the ultimate compliment by telling her that she is able to take the place of Rome.

92. The relationship started in an unknown year in the reign of Domitian, for in 8.45 Martial refers to the fact that Terentius Priscus had been restored to him from Sicily. For the possibility that other Prisci in Martial's

epigrams are referring to Terentius Priscus, see the various responses of Howell, "Martial's Return" 174–76; Nauta 69.

93. See Sullivan, *Martial* 55.

94. I have kept the numbering of Shackleton Bailey's Loeb edition; in older editions and academic discussions the epigram is numbered as 10.19.

95. The association of Cato and the theater goes back to an incident where Cato felt the urge to leave the theater during the Floralia when the mime actresses did their traditional striptease.

96. In reality Pliny was not as serious as Martial makes him out to be. In one of his letters he refers to light verse that he writes in his free time (Pliny the Younger, *Letters* 4.14). Elsewhere he reveals that his inspiration for writing these came from none other than Cicero, who engaged in the same pursuit (*Letters* 7.4).

97. The translation is that of Betty Radice in the Loeb edition of Pliny's Letters. Scholars on Martial have been overwhelmingly positive in their assessment of Pliny's letter. Garthwaite ("Patronage" 163) calls Pliny a professed admirer of Martial's epigrams. Scholars on Pliny respond somewhat differently. Marchesi (65) calls Pliny's assessment of Martial's work "(deceptively) condescending."

98. The quote comes from Santoro L'Hoir 157, who must also be credited with the idea to draw up a comparison between Pliny and Cicero.

## *Commentaries on Individual Books of Epigrams*

### *Sorted by book number*

Coleman, Kathleen M., ed. *M. Valerii Martialis Liber Spectaculorum*. New York: Oxford University Press, 2006.

Citroni, Mario, ed. *M. Valerii Martialis Epigrammaton liber I*. Florence: La nuova Italia, 1975.

Howell, Peter, ed. *A Commentary on Book One of the Epigrams of Martial*. London: Athlone, 1980.

Williams, Craig A., ed. *Martial: Epigrams Book Two*. New York: Oxford University Press, 2004.

Fusi, Alessandro, ed. *M. Valerii Martialis: Epigrammaton liber tertius*. Hildesheim: Olms, 2006.

Moreno Soldevila, Rosario, ed. *Martial, Book IV: A Commentary*. Boston: Brill, 2006.

Howell, Peter, ed. *Martial: Epigrams V*. Warminster, UK: Aris & Phillips, 1995.

Canobbio, Alberto, ed. *M. Valerii Martialis: Epigrammaton liber quintus.* Naples: Loffredo, 2011.

Grewing, Farouk, ed. *Martial, Buch VI: Ein Kommentar*. Göttingen: Vandenhoeck & Ruprecht, 1997.

Galán Vioque, Guillermo. *Martial, Book VII: A Commentary*. Translated by J. J. Zoltowski. Boston: Brill, 2002.

Schöffel, Christian, ed. *Martial, Buch 8: Einleitung, Text, Übersetzung, Kommentar*. Stuttgart: F. Steiner, 2002.

Henriksén, Christer, ed. *A Commentary on Martial, Epigrams Book 9*. Oxford: Oxford University Press, 2012.

Damschen, Gregor, and Andreas Heil, eds. *Marcus Valerius Martialis, Epigrammaton liber decimus: Das zehnte Epigrammbuch*. Frankfurt: Lang, 2004.

Kay, N. M., ed. *Martial, Book XI: A Commentary*. London: Duckworth, 1985.

Leary, T. J., ed. *Martial, Book XIII: The Xenia*. London: Duckworth, 2001.

———, ed. *Martial, Book XIV: The Apophoreta*. London: Duckworth, 1996.

# Bibliography

Ahl, F. "Lucan's *De incendio urbis, Epistulae ex Campaniae* and Nero's Ban." *Transactions of the American Philological Association* 102 (1971): 1–27.

Albrecht, Michael von. *A History of Roman Literature: From Livius Andronicus to Boethius*. 2 vols. Boston: Brill, 1997.

Ascher, L. "Was Martial Really Unmarried?" *Classical World* 70 (1977): 441–44.

Barnes, T. D. "The Horoscope of L. Licinius Sura." *Phoenix* 30 (1976): 76–79.

Bell, Albert A., Jr. "Martial's Daughter?" *Classical World* 78 (1984): 21–24.

Bowersock, G. W. *Augustus and the Greek World*. Oxford: Clarendon Press, 1965.

Bridge, R. T., and E. D. C. Lake, eds. *Select Epigrams of Martial*. Oxford: Clarendon Press, 1906.

Buchheit, V. "Martials Beitrag zum Geburtstag Lucans als Zyklus." *Philologus* 105 (1961): 90–96.

———. "Statius' Geburtstagsgedicht zu Ehren Lucans." *Hermes* 88 (1960): 231–49.

Buttrey, Theodore V. "Domitian, the Rhinoceros, and the Date of Martial's *Liber de spectaculis*." *Journal of Roman Studies* 97 (2007): 101–12.

Cameron, A. D. E. "Crinagoras and the Elder Julia." *Liverpool Classical Monthly* 5 (1980): 129–30.

Coleman, K. M. "Martial Book 8 and the Politics of AD 93." In *Papers of the Leeds International Latin Seminar*, vol. 10, edited by Francis Cairns and M. Heath, 337–57. Leeds: F. Cairns, 1998.

Collins, Andrew W. "The Palace Revolution: The Assassination of Domitian and the Accession of Nerva." *Phoenix* 63 (2009): 73–106.

Cowan, Robert. "Fingering Cestos: Martial's Catullus' Callimachus." In *Flavian Poetry and its Greek Past*, edited by Antony Augoustakis, 345–73. Boston: Brill, 2014.

Curchin, Leonard A. *The Romanization of Central Spain: Complexity, Diversity, and Change in a Provincial Hinterland.* New York: Routledge, 2004.

Davies, Penelope J. E. *Death and the Emperor: Roman Imperial Funerary Monuments from Augustus to Marcus Aurelius.* Austin: University of Texas Press, 2004.

Edwards, Catharine. *Death in Ancient Rome.* New Haven, CT: Yale University Press, 2007.

Fear, A. T. "A Latin Master from Roman Spain." *Greece & Rome* 42 (1995): 57–69.

Fearnley, Hannah. "Reading the Imperial Revolution: Martial, *Epigrams* 10." In *Flavian Rome: Culture, Image, Text*, edited by A. J. Boyle and W. J. Dominik, 613–35. Boston: Brill, 2003.

Fitzgerald, William. *Martial: The World of the Epigram.* Chicago: University of Chicago Press, 2007.

Flower, Harriet I. *The Art of Forgetting: Disgrace and Oblivion in Roman Political Culture.* Chapel Hill: University of North Carolina Press, 2006.

Garthwaite, John. "Domitian and the Court Poets Martial and Statius." PhD diss., Cornell University, 1978.

———. "*Ludimus innocui*: Interpreting Martial's Imperial Epigrams." In *Writing Politics in Imperial Rome*, edited by William J. Dominik, John Garthwaite, and Paul A. Roche, 405–27. Boston: Brill, 2009.

———. "The Panegyrics of Domitian in Martial Book 9." *Ramus* 22 (1993): 78–102.

———. "Patronage and Poetic Immortality in Martial, Book 9." *Mnemosyne* 51 (1998): 161–76.

————. "Putting a Price on Praise: Martial's Debate with Domitian in Book 5." In *Toto notus in orbe: Perspektiven der Martial-Interpretation*, edited by Farouk Grewing, 157–73. Stuttgart: F. Steiner Verlag, 1998.

Gow, A. S. F., and D. L. Page. *The Greek Anthology: The Garland of Philip and Some Contemporary Epigrams*. 2 vols. London: Cambridge University Press, 1968.

————. *The Greek Anthology: Hellenistic Epigrams*. 2 vols. Cambridge: Cambridge University Press, 1965.

Grainger, John D. *Nerva and the Roman Succession Crisis of AD 96–99*. New York: Routledge, 2003.

Gresseth, G. K. "The Quarrel between Lucan and Nero." *Classical Philology* 52 (1957): 24–27.

Griffin, Miriam T. *Nero: The End of a Dynasty*. London: B. T. Batsford Ltd., 1984.

Hemelrijk, Emily. *Matrona Docta: Educated Women in the Roman Elite from Cornelia to Julia Domna*. New York: Routledge, 1999.

Henderson, John. "On Pliny on Martial on Pliny on Anon . . . (*Epistles* 3.21/ *Epigrams* 10.19)." *Ramus* 30 (2001): 56–87.

Holzberg, Niklas. *Martial und das antike Epigramm*. Darmstadt: Wissenschaftliche Buchgesellschaft, 2002.

Howell, Peter. *Martial*. London: Bristol Classical, 2009.

————. "Martial's Return to Spain." In *Toto notus in orbe: Perspektiven der Martial-Interpretation*, edited by Farouk Grewing, 173–87. Stuttgart: F. Steiner Verlag, 1998.

Jones, Brian W. *The Emperor Domitian*. New York: Routledge, 1992.

Keay, S. J. *Roman Spain*. Berkeley: University of California Press, 1988.

Kleijwegt, Marc. "A Question of Patronage: Seneca and Martial." *Acta Classica* 42 (1999): 105–20.

Kokkinos, Nikos. *Antonia Augusta: Portrait of a Great Roman Lady*. New York: Routledge, 1992.

Levick, Barbara. *Vespasian*. New York: Routledge, 1999.

Livingstone, Niall, and Gideon Nisbet. *Epigram*. Cambridge: Cambridge University Press, 2010.

Lorenz, Sven. "Catullus and Martial." In *A Companion to Catullus*, edited by Marilyn B. Skinner, 418–39. Malden, MA: Blackwell, 2007.

————. *Erotik und Panegyrik: Martials epigrammatische Kaiser*. Tübingen: Narr, 2002.

Mackail, J. W. *Latin Literature*. New York: C. Scribner's Sons, 1895.

Mantke, J. "Do We Know Martial's Parents? (Martial V 34)." *Eos* 57 (1967–68): 234–44.

Marchesi, Ilaria. *The Art of Pliny's Letters: A Poetics of Allusion in the Private Correspondence*. New York: Cambridge University Press, 2008.

McGill, Scott. *Plagiarism in Latin Literature*. Cambridge: Cambridge University Press, 2012.

Mierse, William E. *Temples and Towns in Roman Iberia: The Social and Architectural Dynamics of Sanctuary Designs, from the Third Century B.C. to the Third Century A.D.* Berkeley: University of California Press, 1999.

Nauta, Ruurd. *Poetry for Patrons: Literary Communication in the Age of Domitian*. Boston: Brill, 2002.

Neger, Margot. "*'Graece numquid' ait 'poeta nescis?'*: Martial and the Greek Epigrammatic Tradition." In *Flavian Poetry and its Greek Past*, edited by Antony Augoustakis, 327–45. Boston: Brill, 2014.

———. *Martials Dichtergedichte: Das Epigramm als Medium der poetischen Selbstreflexion*. Tübingen: Narr, 2012.

Newlands, Carole, ed. *Statius, Silvae: Book II*. New York: Cambridge University Press, 2011.

Nisbet, Gideon. *Greek Epigram in the Roman Empire: Martial's Forgotten Rivals*. New York: Oxford University Press, 2003.

Noy, David. *Foreigners at Rome: Citizens and Strangers*. Swansea: Classical Press of Wales, 2000.

Nystrom, Bradley, ed. *An English Translation of the Poetry of Lucillius, a First-Century Greek Epigrammatist*. Lewiston, NY: Edwin Mellen Press, 2004.

Post, Edwin, ed. *Selected Epigrams of Martial*. Boston: Ginn & Co., 1908.

Santoro L'Hoir, Francesca. *The Rhetoric of Gender Terms: 'Man,' 'Woman,' and the Portrayal of Character in Latin Prose*. Boston: Brill, 1992.

Seo, J. Mira. "Plagiarism and Poetic Identity in Martial." *American Journal of Philology* 130 (2009): 567–93.

Shackleton Bailey, D. R., ed. and trans. *Martial: Epigrams*. 3 vols. Cambridge, MA: Harvard University Press, 1993.

Sider, David. *The Epigrams of Philodemus: Introduction, Text, and Commentary*. New York: Oxford University Press, 1997.

Southern, Pat. *Domitian: Tragic Tyrant*. Bloomington: Indiana University Press, 1997.

Spisak, Art L. *Martial: A Social Guide*. London: Duckworth, 2007.

Stadter, Philip A. "Introduction: Setting Plutarch in His Context." In *Sage and Emperor: Plutarch, Greek Intellectuals, and Roman Power in the Time of Trajan (98–117 A.D.)*, edited by Philip A. Stadter and Luc van der Stockt, 1–27. Leuven: Leuven University Press, 2002.

Sullivan, J. P. *Martial: The Unexpected Classic*. New York: Cambridge University Press, 1991.

———. "Was Martial Really Married? A Reply." *Classical World* 72 (1979): 238–39.

Swann, Bruce W. *Martial's Catullus: The Reception of an Epigrammatic Rival*. New York: G. Olms, 1994.

———. "*Sic scribit Catullus*: The Importance of Catullus for Martial's Epigrams." In *Toto notus in orbe: Perspektiven der Martial-Interpretation*, edited by Farouk Grewing, 48–59. Stuttgart: F. Steiner Verlag, 1998.

Syme, Ronald. "Curtailed Tenures of Consular Legates." *Zeitschrift für Epigraphik und Papyrologie* 59 (1985): 265–79.

Varner, Eric R. *Mutilation and Transformation: "Damnatio Memoriae" and Roman Imperial Portraiture*. Boston: Brill, 2004.

Watson, Lindsay, and Patricia A. Watson, eds. *Martial: Select Epigrams*. New York: Cambridge University Press, 2003.

Watson, Patricia A. "Martial's Marriage: A New Approach." *Rheinisches Museum für Philologie* 146 (2003): 38–48.

Webb, W. T., ed. *Select Epigrams from Martial for English Readers*. London: Macmillan, 1879.

*Selected Epigrams*

# Book One

## 1.1

Here is the one you read and ask for:
Martial, known the world around
for witty books of epigrams,
whom you, devoted reader, crowned
with fame—while he has life and breath—
such as few poets get in death.

## 1.9

You want to be handsome, Cotta, and yet great—
   but handsome men are always second-rate.

## 1.10

Gemellus wants to marry Maronilla.
He burns, implores, brings gifts, won't be put off.
Is she so pretty? No, there's none more homely.
What makes her so appealing then? Her cough.

## 1.13

When faithful Arria gave her spouse the sword
   she'd drawn from her own flesh, she said, "Believe me,
Paetus, the wound I made gives me no pain;
   it's that which you will give yourself that grieves me."

## 1.16

You'll read some good things here, some fair, more worse.
    There's no way else to make a book of verse.

## 1.17

Titus would have me practice law.
He says, "The field is splendid."
A field is splendid, Titus, if
a *farmer* keeps it tended.

## 1.19

Aelia, I recall you had four teeth.
    One cough knocked two out; one, the other two.
Now you can safely cough the whole day long.
    A third cough can do nothing more to you.

## 1.20

What folly is this? In front of crowds of guests,
    you gobble every mushroom on the plate.
What curse, Caecilianus, suits such greed?
    May you eat mushrooms such as Claudius ate.

## 1.23

You ask to dinner none but those you've bathed with.
    The baths yield all your guests. I used to brood,
Cotta, about why *I* was not invited.
    I know now: you disliked me in the nude.

## 1.24

You see that shag-haired fellow, Decianus,
    who frightens even you with his grim brow,

who talks of heroes—Curii, Camilli?
  Don't trust his looks. He played the bride just now.

## 1.27

Last night, Procillus, after I had drunk
four pints or so, I asked if you would dine
with me today. At once, you thought the matter
was settled, based on statements blurred by wine—
a risky precedent. Good memory
is odious in one who drinks with me.

## 1.28

Whoever thinks Acerra stinks of last night's wine
  is wrong. He drinks till light begins to shine.

## 1.29

Rumor reports that you recite my books
  in public, Fidentinus, as your own.
Call them mine, and I'll send you them for nothing.
  Buy me out if you want them yours alone.

## 1.30

Diaulus was a surgeon; he's an undertaker now—
  starting to practice medicine the best way he knows how.

## 1.32

Sabidius, I don't like you. Why? No clue.
  I just don't like you. That will have to do.

## 1.33

Gellia doesn't weep for her dead father
  when she's alone, but tears pour on command

if someone comes. Who courts praise isn't mourning—
    he truly grieves who grieves with none at hand.

## 1.34

You always sin with doors flung wide, unguarded;
    your intrigues, Lesbia, are unconcealed.
A watcher thrills you much more than a lover;
    you take no joy in joys that aren't revealed.
Yet whores drive watchers off with bolts and curtains;
    few chinks expose Summemmian brothel rooms.
Learn modesty from Chione or Ias;
    even filthy street-whores hide in tombs.
Is my critique too stringent, to your thought?
    I don't say "Don't get fucked," just "Don't get caught."

## 1.37

You take a dump in gold (poor gold!) and aren't ashamed of
    it.
    Bassa, you drink from glass; it therefore costs you more to
    shit.

## 1.38

The book that you recite from, Fidentinus, is my own.
    But when you read it badly, it belongs to you alone.

## 1.40

Spite, do you scowl to read of praise, though due?
    Then envy all, while no one envies you.

## 1.46

When you say, "I'm in haste, so get it done with,"
    my passion droops and falters instantly.

Tell me to wait: held back, I'll just go faster.
    If *you're* in a hurry, Hedylus, don't rush *me*.

## 1.47

Diaulus was a doctor lately; now he's a mortician:
    he does as undertaker what he did as a physician.

## 1.54

If you can spare some time for being loved
(for you have friends on every side, it's true),
Fuscus, make room for me, if space remains.
Do not refuse me just because I'm new:
your old friends all were new once. See if you
can't make a newfound chum an old friend, too.

## 1.57

Flaccus, you ask what kind of girl I want?
    One not too hard to get, but not too easy.
I like a girl between the two extremes:
    one who will neither satiate nor tease me.

## 1.58

The dealer priced a boy at a hundred grand.
    I laughed, but Phoebus paid it instantly.
My cock is grieved and grumbles to himself,
    applauding Phoebus and berating me.
But *his* cock earned two million for him. Score
    as much for me, cock: next time I'll pay more.

## 1.59

The dole at Baiae matches that in Rome.
    Why amidst pleasures does such hunger dwell?

Give me the murky baths of Lupus and Gryllus:
    why dine so badly, Flaccus, to bathe well?

## 1.62

Laevina, no less chaste than ancient Sabines
    and sterner than her mate (who was quite dire),
on trusting Lakes Lucrinus and Avernus
    and warming in the Baian spas, caught fire,
ran off with a youth, and left her spouse bereft:
    arriving, Penelope; Helen when she left.

## 1.63

You'd have me recite my poems. I decline.
    You want to recite *yours*, Celer, not hear mine.

## 1.64

You're lovely, yes, and young, it's true,
and rich—who can deny your wealth?
But you aren't lovely, young, or rich,
Fabulla, when you praise yourself.

## 1.71

I'll drink six drafts for Laevia and seven for Justina,
    five for Lycis, four for Lyde, and for Ida, three.
Let all my girls be numbered by the pouring of Falernian,
    and since not one of them has come, let you, Sleep, come to
      me.

## 1.72

You think yourself a poet, Fidentinus,
based on *my* verse, and want it widely known?
So Aegle thinks she has her teeth because
she purchased Indian ivory and bone;
so too Lycoris, blacker than ripe mulberries,
when powdered with white lead thinks she looks fair.

And you, the same way you've become a poet,
when you've gone bald, will have a head of hair.

## 1.73

None in all Rome would've wished to touch your wife
        for free—if you permitted it—not ever.
Now that you've posted guards, Caecilianus,
        you've drawn a crowd of fuckers. You're so clever.

## 1.74

He was your lover, Paula. It's a fact you could deny.
        Look, he's now your husband. Can you *still* call it a lie?

## 1.77

Charinus has good health, and yet he's pale.
Charinus doesn't drink much, yet he's pale.
Charinus can digest well, yet he's pale.
Charinus gets some sun, and yet he's pale.
Charinus paints his face, and yet he's pale.
Charinus licks a cunt, and yet he's pale.

## 1.83

Manneia, your lapdog licks your lips with his tongue.
        It's no surprise that a dog likes eating dung.

## 1.84

Though Quirinalis doesn't want a mate,
he does want sons. He's found a way to get them.
He fucks his slave girls, filling his estate
and house in town chock-full of homegrown knights:
a real paterfamilias, by his lights.

## 1.89

Cinna, you're always murmuring in one's ear—
even what's safe to chatter in a crowd.

You laugh, complain, blame, judge, and weep in one's ear;
you sing in one's ear, keep still, and shout out loud.
This malady is so ingrained in you,
you often whisper praise of Caesar, too.

## 1.90

Bassa, I never saw you close to men;
    no gossip linked you to a lover here.
A crowd of your own sex was always with you
    at every function, no man coming near.
I have to say, I thought you a Lucretia,
    but you (for shame!) were fucking even then.
You dare to link twin cunts and, with your monstrous
    clitoris, pretend to fuck like men.
You'd suit a Theban riddle perfectly:
    where there's no man, there's still adultery.

## 1.91

You blast my verses, Laelius; yours aren't shown.
    Either don't carp at mine or show your own.

## 1.94

Aegle, when you were fucked, your singing sucked.
Now you're a vocalist, but can't be kissed.

## 1.95

You shout down lawyers, Aelius, without cease,
    but not for free. You're paid to hold your peace.

### 1.102

Lycoris, the painter of your Venus tried,
I'd say, to show he's on Minerva's side.

## 1.105

Wine born, Ovidius, in Nomentan fields,
    after a lengthy lapse of time occurs,

puts off its name and nature in old age,
    and the old jar's called whatever it prefers.

## 1.106

Rufus, you often add more water
to your wine. If friends insist,
you'll sip an ounce of wine, half-drowned.
Has Naevia pledged a night of bliss
and you would keep your fucking sure,
your mischief clear? You sigh, keep still,
and groan: she's turned you down. Then drink
full cups of unmixed wine to kill
your bitter grief. Why should you keep
yourself deprived? You have to sleep.

## 1.108

You have a house (and may it stand and prosper
    for many years) that's lovely to behold,
but over the Tiber, while my garret views
    Vipsanian laurels. Here I have grown old.
Gallus, I'd have to move to call each morning.
    That's hard, though were it farther still, I'd go.
But you have little need for one more client,
    while it means much to me to tell you no.
I'll greet you often at dinner, face to face.
    Mornings, my book will greet you in my place.

## 1.110

"Write shorter epigrams" is your advice.
    Yet you write nothing, Velox. How concise!

## 1.111

Your wisdom is as famed as your devotion;
    your faith and honor, Regulus, are unswerving.
Who wonders that you're sent this book with incense
    does not know how to give to the deserving.

## 1.112

Not knowing you, I'd "Lord" and "Patron" you.
    I've got your number now: "Priscus" will do.

## 1.113

Reader, if you would spend good hours badly,
wasting free time with what I wrote in play
as a young man and boy once, you may seek it
(rubbish I hardly recognize today)
from Quintus Pollius Valerianus,
who will not let my trifles fade away.

## 1.117

Each time we meet, you say right off,
"May I send a boy to get your book
of epigrams? I'll send it back
at once, after I've had a look."
Lupercus, spare the boy; my home,
At the Pear Tree, is far. There I
live three flights up—and steep ones, too.
What you desire is closer by.
Surely you stroll down Argiletum:
facing Caesar's Forum, where
a shop has doorposts crammed with lists
of all the poets—seek me there.
Ask for Atrectus (he's the owner).
From cubby one or two, he'll hand
you Martial, smoothed and purple-clad,
for five denarii, on demand.
You say, "You're not worth such expense"?
Lupercus, you're a man of sense.

# Book Two

## 2.3

Sextus, you have no debts—no debts, I say,
    for one cannot have debts who cannot pay.

## 2.4

How doting is your conduct toward your mother,
and, Ammianus, how she dotes on you!
You call her "sister" and she calls you "brother."
But why do naughty names attract you two?
Why aren't you happy being what you are?
Do you suppose that this is harmless fun?
It's not: a mother who would be a sister
is not content with being either one.

## 2.5

May I fall ill if I don't yearn to see
    you, Decianus, night and day, but you
live two miles off, and when I must return,
    the distance turns to four miles, not just two.
You're often out. When home, you say you're not;
    you need free time; your cases must be planned.
I don't mind going two miles just to see you;
    it's going four to miss you I can't stand.

## 2.10

You kiss me, Postumus, with half your lips.
　　That's fine! Take half away from *that* half, too.
Would you give more, a gift beyond description?
　　Then keep the whole remaining half for you.

## 2.12

Your kisses smell of myrrh; you always have
　　an odor not your own—what must I think?
To smell good all the time appears suspicious.
　　Postumus, men who *always* smell good, stink.

## 2.13

Both judge and lawyer grab what they can get,
so, Sextus, my advice is—pay your debt.

## 2.15

Hormus, you pass your cup to nobody.
That isn't arrogance; it's courtesy.

## 2.17

A female barber sits at Subura's entrance
where torturers hang up their bloody whips
and Argiletum throngs with many a cobbler.
This barber, Ammianus, doesn't clip.
No, she's no clipper; she's a highway robber.

## 2.19

You think a dinner, Zoilus, makes me happy?
　　What's more, a dinner *you* provide? Some hope!
The guest who's happy with a meal of yours
　　should lie with beggars on Aricia's slope.

## 2.20

Paulus buys verse, which he recites as his,
　　for if the things you buy aren't yours, what is?

## 2.21

Some get your hand: some, kisses. You demand,
    "Which would you like? You choose." I'll take the hand.

## 2.22

What use are you, Apollo and the Muses?
    See how the playful Muse afflicts her poet:
Postumus gave me a half-lipped kiss before;
    he's started using *both* lips to bestow it.

## 2.23

"Who's Postumus in your book?" you ask
repeatedly, but I won't tell.
Why should I make those kissings mad
that can avenge themselves so well?

## 2.25

Galla, you say you will, then break your vow.
    So, if you always lie, refuse me now.

## 2.26

Bithynicus, since Naevia breathes in gasps
    and coughs hard, often sending spittle flying
into your lap, you think you've got it made?
    You're wrong: she's playing up to you, not dying.

## 2.27

When Selius, praising you, spreads nets for dinner,
    bring him to hear you read or plead a case.
"That's it!" "Great!" "Zinger!" "Wicked!" "Bravo!" "Brilliant!"
    "Well said!"—"The dinner's yours now; shut your face."

## 2.28

If someone says you're sodomized, Sextillus,
    give him your middle finger with loud laughter.
You neither fuck nor bugger; the hot mouth

of Vetustina isn't what you're after.
  You don't do these. What then? I can't explain.
    But you know two more options still remain.

## 2.30

I chanced to seek a loan of twenty thousand—
  which one could give away and not think twice.
The man I asked, a trusted longtime friend,
  whose strongbox whips up riches in a trice,
said, "Be a lawyer. You'll make piles of cash."
  I asked for money, Gaius, not advice.

## 2.31

I've often fucked Chrestina. You ask, "How was it?"
  If, Marianus, it *can* be done, she does it.

## 2.33

Philaenis, why don't I kiss you? You are bald.
Philaenis, why don't I kiss you? You are red.
Philaenis, why don't I kiss you? You've one eye.
Whoever kisses these is giving head.

## 2.38

What yield does my Nomentan farmstead bear?
  Linus, I don't see *you* when I am there.

## 2.39

You give a known adulteress gowns of violet and scarlet.
  Give her a gift she's merited: the toga of a harlot.

## 2.42

Washing your ass pollutes the tub. Instead,
    to make it fouler, Zoilus, douse your head.

## 2.49

I won't wed Telesina: she's a tart.
    But she sleeps with boys. I've had a change of heart.

## 2.50

You suck and drink water, Lesbia—so you should:
    you take in water where it does most good.

## 2.51

Often your strongbox holds just one denarius,
    Hyllus, and that's rubbed smoother than your ass.
No barkeeper or baker will obtain it,
    but one whose outsize penis is first-class.
Your belly watches as your asshole dines,
    one gorging as the wretched other pines.

## 2.52

Dasius counts his bathers well. He made
    busty Spatale pay for three. She paid.

## 2.53

You want to be a free man? You're a liar,
    Maximus; you don't. But if you do,
here's how: if you can give up dining out,

   if Veii's grape subdues your thirst, if you
can laugh at wretched Cinna's gold-trimmed dishes
     and wear togas like mine contentedly,
if you use two-bit whores and can't stand straight
     while entering your home, you will be free.
If you've the strength of will to face such things,
     you'll live a freer man than Parthia's kings.

## 2.54

Linus, what deeds your wife suspects,
which part of you she'd have more chaste,
she's shown by blatant signs: she's placed
a eunuch to keep watch on you.
What a malicious, sharp-nosed shrew!

## 2.55

I wished to love you; you would have
me court you. What you want must be.
But if I court you, as you ask,
Sextus, you'll get no love from me.

## 2.56

The Libyans, Gallus, call your wife bad names.
   She's charged with boundless greed—without a doubt,
a foul reproach. Those tales, though, are sheer lies.
   She isn't on the take; she just puts out.

## 2.58

You mock my toga; yours is sleek and fine.
   Mine may be threadbare, Zoilus, but it's mine.

## 2.59

I'm called "The Crumb," a little banquet hall:
   you view the Caesars' tomb from me on high.
Pound couches; call for roses, wine, and nard.
   The god himself reminds you, you will die.

# 2.60

Young Hyllus, you fuck the wife of an armed tribune,
    fearing no worse than that he'll bugger you.
He'll geld you while you sport. "But that's forbidden,"
    you'll say. So it's permitted, what you do?

# 2.61

When your young cheeks first bloomed with hints of down,
    your shameless tongue licked men below the waist.
Now that your vile head's scorned by undertakers,
    and torturers regard you with distaste,
your mouth has a new use: consumed with envy,
    at any name you hear you bark and scoff.
Your noxious tongue should stick to genitals,
    for it was cleaner when it sucked men off.

# 2.62

You pluck your chest and legs and arms; your cock
    is shaved and ringed with short hairs. These you cut,
we know, to please your mistress, Labienus.
    For whose sake do you depilate your butt?

# 2.63

On the Sacred Way, your final hundred thousand
    bought Leda, Milichus. Love at such expense
would be excessive were you rich. You say,
    "I'm not in love." That's *more* extravagance.

# 2.65

Why is Saleianus looking sadder?
"For no small cause," you say, "I've lost my wife."
O monstrous crime of fate! What rotten luck!
Has *she*, rich Secundilla, lost her life,
who brought a dowry of a million, too?
I'm sorry things turned out like that for you.

# 2.66

In Lalage's coiffure, a single ringlet
    was out of place, attached by a loose pin.
Plecusa was struck down, the cruel hair's victim,
    felled with the mirror that revealed the sin.
Cease, Lalage, to fix your baleful hair,
    and may your mad head let no slave girl near it.
Let curling irons brand or razors bare it
    so that your mirror's image shows your spirit.

# 2.67

Wherever you meet me, Postumus, at once
    you cry "How are you doing?" This you call
even if we should meet ten times an hour.
    I think *you* don't do anything at all.

# 2.68

Don't say I'm insolent to greet you now
not as "my lord" or "patron," but by name.
My cap of freedom cost me all I have.
He should have lords and patrons who can't claim
to own himself, and who desires the things
that lords and patrons want. If you can do
without a servant, Olus, then it follows
that you can do without a patron, too.

# 2.70

You don't like others bathing first.
Why, Cotilus, unless you dread
soaking in water that's licked cocks?
But even washing first, you're forced
to wash your cock before your head.

## 2.71

Caecilianus, no one could be kinder.
    Whenever I read epigrams of mine,
you reel off some by Marsus or Catullus.
    Is this a favor, done to make mine shine
compared to lesser poems? That may be.
    I'd rather you recite *your* poetry.

## 2.73

"I don't know what I'm doing," Lyris claims when drunk.
    The same thing she does sober: sucking spunk.

## 2.76

You gave him nothing; Marius bequeathed you
    five whole pounds of silver. He deceived you!

## 2.78

Where to keep fish in summertime, you ask?
    Your so-called "heated baths" would suit the task.

## 2.79

Only when *I've* invited guests, do you ask *me* to dine.
    Today I dine in, Nasica. *So* sorry to decline.

## 2.80

Fannius, fleeing his foes, chose suicide.
    That's crazy—so as not to die, he died!

## 2.83

Husband, you maimed your wife's poor lover.
Shorn of its nose and ears, his face
looks vainly for its former grace.

Do you believe you've done enough?
You're wrong. He still can be sucked off.

## 2.87

Sextus, their love for you makes beauties simmer—
    say you, with the face of an underwater swimmer.

## 2.88

You recite no verse, Mamercus, but claim you write.
    Claim what you like—so long as you don't recite.

## 2.89

Gaurus, you like to stay up all night drinking.
    I pardon it—Cato had that vice, too.
You write verse without Phoebus and the Muses.
    You should be praised—so Cicero would do.
You vomit like Antony, squander like Apicius.
    You suck—I wonder whose bad habit *this* is.

## 2.92

He who alone could grant it gave the Right
of Fathers of Three Children in reward
for poetry I've written. Farewell, wife.
I mustn't waste the bounty of our lord.

## 2.93

"If this book is the second, where's the first?"
    What can I do if *that* one is more shy?
But if you'd rather this become the first one,
    Regulus, dock the title of one *I*.

# Book Three

## 3.3

While black salve hides your fair face, you insult
    the water with your ugly body. Please
believe, through me, the goddess tells you: "Either
    reveal your face, or bathe in a chemise."

## 3.6

May eighteenth should be honored, Marcellinus,
    doubly in your observance: first it gave
the date your father entered heaven's light;
    now first fruits from the downy cheeks you shave.
Although it gave him a fine gift before—
    a happy life—it never gave him more.

## 3.8

Quintus loves Thais. "Which?" The one-eyed one.
    Thais, at least, has one eye; *he* has none.

## 3.9

Cinna, they say, writes verse attacking me.
    He doesn't write, whose verses none will see.

## 3.12

You gave your guests good scent last night,
I grant you, but no food was carved.
How droll, to be perfumed and starved!
To be anointed and not fed
is fine, Fabullus—for the dead.

## 3.14

Famished Tuccius came from Spain.
   Just outside of Rome
at the Mulvian Bridge, he heard the dole
   had ended. He went home.

## 3.15

Cordus gives more on credit than any other.
   "But how? He's poor." He's blind and he's a lover.

## 3.17

A cheese tart, passed around and around the table,
   burned our hands cruelly with its searing heat.
Sabidius' greed burned hotter, so at once
   he blew on it three or four times. Though the treat
cooled down, appearing ready to permit
   our grasp, no one could touch it. It was shit.

## 3.18

Your preface grumbled that your throat was sore.
   You've made your excuses, Maximus. Why say more?

## 3.22

You'd spent twice thirty million on your belly,
Apicius, and ten million more was left.
That was like thirst and famine. Loath to endure
such hardship, you took poison, your last draft.
In no act were you more the epicure.

## 3.26

None, Candidus, but you has land and cash.
    No other owns gold plate and murrine stone,
or vintage Caecuban and Massic wines.
    Talent and judgment, too, are yours alone.
You alone have it all—I don't demur—
    except your wife, for everyone has her.

## 3.27

You often come when asked, but don't invite me.
    I pardon you—if you treat all the same.
Yet others you invite. We both have faults:
    I have no judgment, Gallus; you, no shame.

## 3.28

You seem surprised that Marius' ear smells rank.
    You chat in it, Nestor. He has you to thank.

## 3.32

I can't do crones. Matrinia, do you grumble?
    I *can*, but you're a corpse, not just a crone.

I can do Hecuba and Niobe,
    but not once one's a bitch and one's a stone.

# 3.33

I like a freeborn girl; if that's denied me,
    my next choice is a girl who's been set free.
A slave's my last choice, but if her appearance
    beats theirs, she'll be a freeborn girl to me.

# 3.34

Your name means "snow." It does and doesn't hit the mark.
    You're Chione and you're not: you're cold and dark.

# 3.37

Wealthy friends, you're quick to take offense.
    It's not good manners, but it saves expense.

# 3.39

One-eyed Lycoris loves a boy
    as fine as Ganymede of Troy.
Faustinus, anyone can tell—
    with just one eye, she sees quite well.

# 3.41

Because from your vast riches, Telesinus,
    you loaned me a hundred and fifty grand, you then
assume you're a great friend. *You* great, for giving?
    No, *I*—because you get it back again.

# 3.43

You dye your hair, Laetinus, to feign youth—
  a swan before, a raven now instead.
You don't fool all. Proserpina can tell
  you're gray. She'll pull that mask right off your head.

# 3.45

Whether Apollo fled Thyestes' dinner,
  I can't say. Ligurinus, yours we flee.
The feasts are lavish and superb, but nothing
  can please when you recite your poetry.
I don't want turbot or mullet when we sup;
  I don't want mushrooms or oysters. Just shut up.

# 3.48

Olus, to build a "pauper's cell," sold land.
  A pauper's cell is now at his command.

# 3.49

You mix Veientan for me, while *you* drink Massic wine.
  I'd rather smell your cups than drink from mine.

# 3.51

When I admire your face and legs and hands,
  "You'll like me better nude," you always tease.
Yet, Galla, you won't bathe with me in public.
  Am *I* the one you fear will fail to please?

## 3.53

I wouldn't miss your face and neck
and hands and legs and ass and breasts
and hips and (not to list the rest
by item)—Chloe, I could do
just fine without the whole of you.

## 3.54

I can't afford the price you're asking, so
    to keep things simpler, Galla, just say no.

## 3.55

Wherever you go, we think that Cosmus, moving shop,
    has spilled a vial of cinnamon oil. You should
not pride yourself on foreign nonsense, Gellia.
    That stuff, you know, can make my *dog* smell good.

## 3.57

Lately in dry Ravenna, my sly barkeep proved a cheat:
    I asked for water in my wine; the wine he sold was neat.

## 3.61

Vile Cinna, you ask for "nothing"—so say you.
    If that's true, I deny you nothing, too.

## 3.64

The Sirens, gleeful scourge of mariners,
beguiling bane and cruelhearted joy,
whom no man could abandon once he'd heard them,
were left, they say, through sly Ulysses' ploy.
I'm not surprised; amazement *would* prevail
if he deserted Canius midtale.

## 3.65

An apple's fragrance as a young girl bites it;
    Corycian saffron's odor; the lush scents
of blooming grapevines white with their first clusters
    or grass just cropped by sheep; the redolence
of myrtle, Arab spice-reapers, rubbed amber,
    fire pale with clouds of Eastern incense, soil
lightly sprinkled with summer rain, a garland
    resting on tresses moist with spikenard oil—
your kiss is scented, cruel boy, so sweetly.
    What if you gave it freely and completely?

## 3.68

Lady, thus far I wrote this book for you.
    For whom did I write the latter part? For me.
In this part are the gym, warm baths, the track.
    Withdraw: we're stripping. Don't look or you'll see
nude men. From here on, drunk Terpsichore,
    not knowing what she says, lays shame aside
after the wine and roses, naming bluntly
    what Venus in August welcomes back with pride,
what stewards set as the garden's guard, what virgins
    view from behind a hand. If I know you,
weary of this long book, you'd set it down,
    but now you will be keen to read it through.

## 3.69

All of your epigrams use decent language.
    There's no cock in your verses. That's impressive!
I praise you: you're the purest of the pure.
    There's not a page of mine that's not suggestive.
Let naughty youths and easy girls read mine,

or old men plagued by a mistress and her ploys.
    *Your* words, Cosconius, so pure and pious,
        ought to be read by maidens and young boys.

## 3.70

Aufidia's spouse before, you're now her lover;
        your former rival is the one she wed.
Why want her not as *your* wife, but another's?
        Does it take fear to make you rise in bed?

## 3.71

Your boy's cock hurts; your ass aches. I'm no seer,
        but what you're doing, Naevolus, is clear.

## 3.72

You want to be fucked, but not to bathe with me.
        You must have some great shame that I don't know.
Saufeia, either your breasts hang flat as rags
        or you're afraid your belly's folds will show;
or your split crotch reveals a deep crevasse,
        or something juts outside your pussy's slit.
But no, I'm sure you're gorgeous in the nude.
        If that's true, you've a worse fault: you're a twit.

## 3.73

You sleep with well-hung boys; what stands for them
won't stand for you. So what should I conclude,
Phoebus? I'd like to think that you're a pansy,
but rumor says you don't like being screwed.

# 3.76

You scorn girls, Bassus, and get hard for crones.
    Not beauty but senescence pleases you.
Isn't this madness? Isn't your cock insane?
    Andromache, no, but Hecuba you'd do!

# 3.79

Sertorius starts all things, completing none.
    I reckon when he fucks, he doesn't come.

# 3.80

Apicius, you don't badmouth anyone—
    yet rumor says you have a wicked tongue.

# 3.83

"Make your poems briefer," you exhort.
    "Do me like Chione." Cordus, that's too short!

# 3.84

What says your wife's adulteress?—speaking of
your tongue, Gongylion, not a ladylove.

# 3.86

Chaste lady, I warned you not to read this part
    of my lewd book, but, look!—you're reading still.
Yet if you watch Panniculus and Latinus—
    *these* are no worse than mimes are—read your fill.

# 3.87

Rumor claims your cunt has not been fucked,
    that nothing's purer, Chione, than that place.
And yet you hide the wrong part when you bathe.
    For shame! Transfer that loincloth to your face.

# 3.88

One brother licks a dick; his twin, a twat.
    So are the twins identical or not?

# 3.89

Eat mallows and lettuce, Phoebus; they'd be fitting—
    your face looks like you're straining hard while shitting.

# 3.90

Galla wants me and doesn't. I've no clue,
    given she does and doesn't, *what* she'll do.

# 3.94

You call for a whip, declaring the hare's too rare.
    Rufus, you'd rather cut your cook than your hare.

# 3.96

You do not fuck my girl, you lick her snatch,
yet talk like a stud and fucker. If I catch
you, though, Gargilius, you'll shut your hatch.

# 3.100

Rufus, I sent your courier back at noon.
    He brought my poems sopping wet, I'd say,
for the sky was hurling down torrential rain.
    That book deserved to be sent no other way.

# Book Four

## 4.6

You wish, Malisianus, to seem more chaste
than a shamefaced virgin, but your cheek is worse
than one who—right in Stella's home!—recites
books in the meter of Tibullus' verse.

## 4.7

Why, Hyllus, withhold today what yesterday
　　you gave, so lately kind and now so cold?
Yet now you plead your beard and years and hair.
　　What a long night, if one night makes you old!
Why mock me? Hyllus, tell me in what way
　　did yesterday's boy become a man today?

## 4.12

Thais, you turn down none. Should that not bother you,
　　feel shame at *this*: there's nothing you won't do.

## 4.13

Claudia Peregrina weds my Pudens.
　　Bless your torches, Hymen! Let them shine!
So aptly nard is mixed with cinnamon,
　　and Theseus' honeycombs with Massic wine.
So well weak vines are joined to elms; the lotus

loves water thus, while myrtle loves the shore.
Fair Harmony, dwell always in their bed,
    and Venus bless the couple evermore.
Let her still love him when he's old someday;
    may she seem young to him, even when she's gray.

## 4.15

Caecilianus, when you asked me lately
    to lend you a thousand for a week, I said,
"I'm broke." But now "because a friend is coming,"
    you ask for a dish and serving tools instead.
Are you a fool? Am I, my friend? When I've
    denied you one grand, will I give you five?

## 4.16

Rumor alleged you weren't your stepmom's stepson,
    Gallus, while she was still your father's spouse.
But none could prove it while he was alive.
    Now that he's gone, she's living in your house.
Though Cicero be called from the shades below
    and Regulus himself defend you, none
could clear you: she who won't stop being a stepmom
    after the father's death was never one.

## 4.17

You tell me to write verse about Lycisca
to make her blush and make her angry, too.
Paulus, what a wicked man you are:
you want to have her sucking only you.

## 4.20

Caerellia says she's old, though she's a doll.
    Gellia says she's young, though she's a hag.

Collinus, one can't stomach either one:
    one makes you laugh; the other makes you gag.

## 4.21

Segius claims there are no gods, the skies
are bare. He proves it, too: while he denies
the gods exist, he sees his fortune rise.

## 4.22

New to the marriage bed, not yet accustomed
    to a husband, Cleopatra plunged within
a bright pool, fleeing embraces. But the water
    revealed her, hiding. Under it, her skin
still shone. So lilies under glass are counted;
    so see-through crystal won't let roses hide.
I jumped in, dove, and seized reluctant kisses:
    further embrace the limpid pool denied.

## 4.24

She's buried every friend she's had in life—
    I wish Lycoris would befriend my wife.

## 4.26

I haven't paid you morning calls all year.
    Postumus, shall I say how much I've lost?
Sixty sesterces, maybe thirty. Sorry,
    I buy my toga at a higher cost.

## 4.27

Often you praise my little books, Augustus.
    Envy denies it. Is it then less true?
You've honored me not just with words, but gifts
    that could be granted me by none but you.

See! Envy chews his blackened nails once more.
    Give further, Caesar: make him really sore.

# 4.29

Their number, my dear Pudens, hurts my books;
    their frequency leaves readers cloyed and tired.
Rare things delight: roses cost more in winter;
    the earliest apples are the most desired;
haughtiness makes a grasping mistress dearer;
    young men avoid the always open door.
Persius in one book scores more than Marsus
    in his whole Amazoniad can score.
So too, when you re-read a book of mine,
    pretend I've only one: then it will shine.

# 4.32

A bee, enclosed within a drop of amber,
    both hides and shines, appearing to be frozen
in honey, an apt reward for all her pains:
    one might think it's the death she would have chosen.

# 4.33

You've bookcases of verse you've labored over.
    Why do you publish nothing? "Once I'm dead,
my heirs will do it." *When*, Sosibianus?
    Already it's high time that you were read.

# 4.34

Who calls your toga "snowy" doesn't lie,
    soiled as it may be, Attalus, to the eye.

# 4.36

Your hair is black, your beard, white, Olus. Why?
    You dye your hair; your beard you cannot dye.

# 4.38

Galla, say no. Some torment makes love stronger.
    But, Galla, don't keep saying no much longer.

# 4.41

Why wrap your neck in wool when you recite?
    To wrap it round our ears would be more right.

# 4.43

I never said you're a pansy, Coracinus.
I'm not so rash and bold, nor prone to lie.
If I've said you're a pansy, Coracinus,
may I make Pontia's flask irate, may I
enrage Metilius' drinking-cup. I swear
by Syrian tumors sent from Cybele,
by Phrygian frenzies. What, then, did I say?
Something slight and paltry, you'll agree,
a well-known fact, and one that you cannot
deny yourself. I said that you lick twat.

# 4.44

This is Vesuvius, green just now with vines;
    here fine grapes loaded brimming vats. These heights
were loved by Bacchus more than Nysa's slopes;
    on this mount, satyrs lately danced their rites.
This home of Venus pleased her more than Sparta;
    this spot the name of Hercules made proud.
All lie engulfed in flames and dismal ashes:
    the gods themselves regret it was allowed.

# 4.47

This plaque of yours is glazed with the device
    of Phaethon. Why wish to fire him twice?

## 4.49

One doesn't fathom epigrams, believe me,
    Flaccus, who labels them mere jokes and play.
He's trifling who writes of savage Tereus' meal
    or yours, queasy Thyestes, or the way
Daedalus fit his boy with melting wings
    or Polyphemus grazed Sicilian flocks.
My little books shun bombast, and my Muse
    won't rave in puffed-up tragedy's long frocks.
"Yet all admire, praise, honor those." Indeed,
    they praise those, I confess, but these they read.

## 4.50

Why call me "old man," Thais? Though you mock,
no man's too old for you to suck his cock.

## 4.51

You didn't own six grand, Caecilianus,
    yet rode a litter carried by six men.
Now that blind Fortune's granted you two million,
    coins burst your purse—and you're on foot again.
What wish suits one whose merits are so rare?
    I pray the gods will give you back your chair.

## 4.56

You'd have me call you kind, Gargilianus,
    for sending gifts to widows and old men?
No one is viler, more obscene than you,
    who dare to call your ruses "presents" when
they're like sly hooks cajoling greedy fish,
    like baits that trap dumb beasts through trickery.
If you can't tell a gift from quid pro quo,
    I'll teach you how they differ: give to me.

# 4.58

You mourn your mate in private; it appears,
    Galla, that you're ashamed you have no tears.

# 4.59

As a snake crawled through weeping poplar boughs,
    across the beast's path flowed an amber drip.
Amazed to be held fast in the thick sap,
    it stiffened, swiftly bound in ice's grip.
Don't, Cleopatra, vaunt your royal tomb:
    a viper lies in a more splendid room.

# 4.63

Caerellia, a mother, bound for Baiae
    from Bauli, drowned, destroyed by a wild sea.
What fame you've squandered, waters! Once, though ordered
    by Nero, you refused this infamy.

# 4.65

Philaenis always weeps from just one eye.
How can that be? She *has* just one—that's why.

# 4.69

You always serve such fine wine, Papylus,
    but rumor makes us pass it up. They say
this flask has widowed you four times. I don't
    believe it—but my thirst has gone away.

# 4.70

His father left him just dry rope
when he drew his final breath.
Who'd have thought Ammianus could
regret his father's death?

# 4.71

I've long searched all of Rome, Safronius Rufus,
    for a girl who would say no. No girl says no,
as if it were a sin or something shameful
    or not allowed. No girl says no. And so
is no one chaste? Yes, thousands. Chaste girls choose
    neither to give their favors nor refuse.

# 4.72

Quintus, you'd have me give my books to you.
    I've none, but Tryphon's shop has a supply.
"Should I pay cash for trash and *buy* your verse?
    I'm no such fool," you tell me. Nor am I.

# 4.75

Nigrina, paragon of Latin brides,
    happy in spirit, happy in your mate,
you're pleased to mix your own wealth with your spouse's,
    glad ally and copartner in his fate.
Evadne burned on her husband's pyre; no less fame
    conveyed Alcestis to the stars above;
but you top both: this sure pledge while you live
    means that you needn't die to prove your love.

# 4.76

You sent six grand; I'd asked for twelve. To score
    the twelve I want, I'll ask for twenty-four.

# 4.77

I never asked the gods for wealth:
my small means brought serene delight.
Sorry, but leave now, poverty!
Why this new prayer? I want to see
Zoilus hang himself for spite.

# 4·79

You've bought the farm in Tibur where you always were my
      guest.
   I've bilked you, Matho: sold you what you already
      possessed.

# 4·81

Fabulla, when she'd read my verse complaining
that *no* girl says no—though her lover pled
once, twice, and thrice with her—ignored his plea.
Fabulla, give your promise now. I said
"say no," but not "say no relentlessly."

# 4·83

Naevolus, when you're free of cares, you're churlish,
      but troubled, you're the best of men. You scorn
us all when you're at ease, don't answer greetings;
      to you, no one's born free—or even born.
Worried, you offer gifts, invite a guest,
      greet him as "lord" and "patron." Stay distressed.

# 4·84

No one in all of Rome can offer
firsthand proof that Thais fucks,
though many long and beg for it.
Is she so chaste, then? No, she sucks.

# 4·85

We drink from glasses, Ponticus, you from stone—
      so we can't see your wine's unlike our own.

# 4·87

Your Bassa always sets a baby near,
      Fabullus, calling it her "pet" and "dear,"

yet — here's the kicker — tots don't warm her heart.
   So what's her motive? Bassa tends to fart.

# Book Five

## 5.2

Matrons, boys, and modest girls,
to you my page is dedicated.
You who are overfond of bolder
mischief, wit unexpurgated,
may read my four licentious books.
The fifth book jests with Caesar, who
may read the verse without a blush—
and in Minerva's presence, too.

## 5.4

Myrtale tends to reek of excess drink.
To fool us she chews bay leaves and combines
neat wine with the sly herbs instead of water.
So, Paulus, when she's flushed, with veins like vines,
every time you see her come your way,
"Myrtale's drunk on laurel," you may say.

## 5.9

I felt unwell. But, Symmachus, you came
    at once and brought a hundred students, too.
A hundred hands, chilled by the north wind, touched me.
    I had no fever then. But now I do.

## 5.17

While speaking, Gellia, about your forebears,
    *their* ancestors, and mighty names, you said
a knight like me was a base match. *You'd* have none
    but a senator; a cop is what you wed.

## 5.20

If you and I, dear Martial, could
enjoy our days, secure from strife,
spending our leisure idly, both
at liberty to relish life,
we wouldn't know the halls and homes
of mighty men, no bitter courts,
no gloomy Forum, no proud busts,
but riding, chatting, books, and sports,
the portico, the shade, the baths,
the fountain—daily, these would be
our haunts, our work. Now neither lives
his life. We feel our good days flee,
numbered and spent. Knowing the way
to live, why should a man delay?

## 5.32

Crispus didn't leave his wife a cent.
    Who was his heir? Himself. It all was spent.

## 5.33

A lawyer slanders my verse. I don't know who—
    but, lawyer, you'll be sorry when I do.

## 5.34

To you, my parents Fronto and Flaccilla,
    I commend this girl, my darling and delight.
Don't let the dark shades and the huge-mouthed hellhound

fill my small Erotion with fright.
She would have known the chill of six midwinters
    had she survived by just as many days.
Now let her lisping mouth prattle my name
    to her old patrons, as she romps and plays.
Let no hard turf hide her soft bones. Earth, do
    not press her harshly; she was light on you.

# 5.36

Faustinus, one I flattered in my book
    pretends he owes me nothing. What a crook!

# 5.42

Sly thieves will smash your coffer and steal your cash;
    impious flames will wreck your family home;
your debtor won't repay your loan or interest;
    your barren fields will yield less than you've sown;
a crafty mistress will despoil your steward;
    a wave will swamp your ships piled high with stores.
But what you give to friends is safe from Fortune:
    only the wealth you give is always yours.

# 5.43

Laecania's teeth are snowy; those of Thais, black with rot.
    The reason? Thais has her own; Laecania's were bought.

# 5.45

Bassa, you say you're beautiful and young.
    Whoever says such things is neither one.

# 5.46

I just like kisses snatched when you're unwilling;
    your anger, not your beauty, turns me on.
To ask you, Diadumenus, I beat you.
    Now both your love and fear of me are gone.

# 5.47

He swears he never dines in. That's no line.
    If not invited, Philo doesn't dine.

# 5.52

I'll always cherish what you've done for me.
    Why don't I speak of it? Because you do.
Whenever I tell someone of your bounty,
    he cries at once: "*He* told me of it, too!"
Some things two can't do well; just one suffices.
    *You* must keep mum if you want *me* to gush.
Believe me, Postumus, the greatest gifts
    are canceled when the giver just won't hush.

# 5.53

Bassus, why write of Medea or Thyestes?
    What's Niobe or Andromache to you?
Deucalion's your best theme (*drown your pages*)
    or Phaethon, if you'd rather (*fire will do*).

# 5.57

When I call you "lord," don't swagger, Cinna. Why?
    I often give your slave the same reply.

# 5.58

You say you'll live tomorrow, always tomorrow.
    When will it get here? Where is it abiding?
How far off, Postumus? Where will you find it?
    Is it in Parthia or Armenia, hiding?
Already it's as old as Priam or Nestor.
    To buy tomorrow, how much would you pay?
Will you live *then*? Today is late already.
    He's wise who did his living yesterday.

# 5.59

In sending you no silver and no gold,
  my purpose, eloquent Stella, is to please.
A lavish giver wants a big return—
  my earthenware will put you at your ease.

# 5.64

Callistus, pour me a double of Falernian.
  Chill it, Alcimus, with summer snows.
Sleek my damp hair with ample oil of cardamom,
  and weight my brows with garlands made of rose.
The Mausoleum of Caesar, so close by,
  says, "Live it up, for even gods can die."

# 5.66

Pontilianus, though often hailed, you never
  greet first. If that's your way, farewell forever.

# 5.68

I sent you hair from northerners up yonder
  to show you, Lesbia, that yours is blonder.

# 5.73

Why, Theodorus, don't I send
my books, though you demand and plead
repeatedly? My reason's good:
so you won't give me *yours* to read.

# 5.74

Asia and Europe cover Pompey's sons,
  but Libyan earth, if any, hides *his* plot.
Why wonder that he's scattered through the world?
  Wreckage so vast can't lie in just one spot.

# 5.75

A law forced Laelia into wedded life—
    so, Quintus, she's rightly called your *lawful* wife.

# 5.76

By drinking poison often, Mithridates
    from all pernicious toxins gained immunity.
So, Cinna, since you always dine so poorly,
    you face down death by famine with impunity.

# 5.79

Eleven times you rose at dinner, Zoilus,
    to change the outfit you were dining in,
so that your sweat-drenched clothing wouldn't cling
    or subtle drafts disturb your rested skin.
Why don't *I* sweat at dinner, as a rule?
    Having one outfit keeps me mighty cool.

# 5.81

If poor, Aemilianus, poor you'll stay.
    None but the rich get wealthier today.

# 5.82

Why did you promise me two hundred grand
    if you can't give me ten? Perhaps you can
but just don't want to? Isn't that more shameful?
    Gaurus, go to hell, you petty man!

# 5.83

I flee you, Dindymus, when chased; I chase you when you flee.
    It's not your wanting me I want; it's your *not* wanting me.

# Book Six

## 6.6

Lupercus, in a comedy
    the actors number only three,
but *four* men win your Paula's heart
    (she even loves the walk-on part).

## 6.12

The hair she swears is hers Fabulla bought.
So, Paulus, is that perjury or not?

## 6.14

Laberius, you claim that you can write
excellent verse. Why don't you, since you can?
If anyone who *can* write good verse *doesn't*,
I'll think he's an extraordinary man.

## 6.15

While an ant wandered in the shade of poplars,
    a drop of amber trapped the tiny beast,
so she who was despised while still alive
    has been made precious now that she's deceased.

## 6.16

You whose sickle frightens men, whose cock
    scares queers, guard this secluded plot with care.

Keep old thieves from your orchard, but let in
    a boy or lovely girl with flowing hair.

## 6.17

Cinnamus, you'd have us call you Cinna.
Isn't that barbarous beyond belief!
So, if your name were Furius before,
we likewise ought to call you Fur, you thief.

## 6.18

In Spanish soil rests pious Saloninus;
    no better soul's seen Styx's home before.
It's wrong to mourn; since you survive him, Priscus,
    part of him lives, the part he valued more.

## 6.20

I asked you for a hundred grand in loan
    after you'd asked what help you could bestow.
For ten days you ask questions, waver, stall,
    and torture us both. Please, Phoebus, just say no.

## 6.22

You're marrying your lover, Proculina,
taking as spouse your partner in transgression
so that the law can't brand you with adultery.
That isn't marrying; it's a confession.

## 6.23

"Stand up!" you always tell my penis, Lesbia.
    A cock's no finger, rising on demand.
Although you urge with coaxing hands and words,
    your face dictates the opposite command.

# 6.24

Carisianus never plays—
he wears a toga on holidays.

# 6.30

If you had promptly given me six thousand
when you said "Take it home; it's yours today,"
I'd feel I owed you for two hundred thousand.
Instead, you gave it after much delay,
seven or nine months later. Want the truth?
Paetus, your six grand was thrown away.

# 6.33

Sabellus the bugger, once the gladdest man,
    is now the saddest, Matho. What bad luck!
Escapes or deaths of slaves, thefts, fires, bereavements
    plague him. Poor man, he's even forced to fuck.

# 6.34

Load me with kisses, Diadumenus.
    You ask "How many?" You would bid me count
the waves, the shells that dot Aegean shores,
    the bees that wander the Cecropian mount,
the cheers and claps that fill the theater
    when Caesar's face comes suddenly into view.
Not the sum Lesbia gave to witty Catullus
    when begged: he who can count them wants too few.

# 6.36

With nose and penis both so large in size,
    you smell it, Papylus, each time you rise.

# 6.40

Lycoris, once no woman could outshine you.
>    Now Glycera's the one none can outdo.
She'll be like you; you cannot be like her.
>    Time does that: her I *want*; I *wanted* you.

# 6.41

Reciting with one's throat wrapped up in fleece
>    shows one can neither speak nor hold one's peace.

# 6.45

You've played enough, you wanton cunts: get married.
>    Chaste love you are allowed and nothing but.
Is this chaste love? Laetoria weds Lygdus.
>    She'll act worse as a wife than as a slut.

# 6.46

The Blues won't run, despite the constant lash—
>    yet, Catianus, still they're earning cash.

# 6.48

When togaed crowds, Pomponius, shout "Bravo!"
>    your dinner, not your speech, has moved them so.

# 6.50

When paying court to good men, Telesinus,
>    a pauper, wore a shabby, threadbare gown.
But since he started seeing filthy queers,
>    he buys up silver, tables, land cash down.
Want to get rich, Bithynicus? Get a clue:
>    chaste kisses bring small gain—or none—to you.

# 6.51

Lupercus, since you dine so much without me,
>    I'll pay you back by being troublesome.

I'm angry: call, send, beg me all you please—
    "What will you do?" What will I do? I'll come.

## 6.52

Here lies Pantagathus, whose life was brief,
    taken in boyhood, to his master's grief.
With steel just skimming skin, he had the skill
    to shave rough cheeks and trim each straying strand.
Be light and kind, earth, as you should; you still
    cannot be lighter than his artful hand.

## 6.53

Andragoras bathed and dined with us with cheer;
    next day, Faustinus, he was found stone dead.
What caused his sudden death, you ask? He dreamed
    Doctor Hermocrates approached his bed.

## 6.55

Because you smell of Niceros' lead boxes,
black with cinnamon and cassia wood
and all the spice nest of the splendid phoenix,
you laugh at us who *don't* smell, Coracinus.
I'd rather smell of nothing than smell good.

## 6.56

You think you've cheated gossip, Charidemus,
    because your legs and chest are rough with hair?
Trust me: remove the hair from your whole body
    and swear an oath you pluck your buttocks bare.
"What for?" You know what many folks have said—
    make them assume you're sodomized instead.

## 6.57

You craft false locks from ointment, Phoebus, hiding
    with painted curls your bald and dirty head.
You needn't call a barber for a haircut:
    a sponge can give a better shave instead.

# 6.59

That it's not cold makes Baccara grieve and gripe
    thanks to his many woolen cloaks. He prays
for murky fog and wind and snow; he hates
    when temperatures turn mild on winter days.
You hard-heart, when has *my* cloak, which a breeze
    can lift from my shoulders, ever done you wrong?
How much more natural and more humane
    to wear your woolen cloaks all August long!

# 6.60

Rome praises, loves, recites my little books.
    I'm carried in each hand or pocket. See!
Someone blushes, pales, gapes, yawns, or hates it.
    That's what I want: my verse now pleases me.

# 6.62

Salanus, a father, lost his only son.
Send presents, Oppianus. Why delay?
Oh, what a wicked shame! What evil Fates!
Which vulture now will make this corpse his prey?

# 6.66

When Gellianus the auctioneer was selling
a girl just now, of none-too-good report,
the kind who sits in the middle of Subura,
for quite a while the bids had fallen short.
Wanting to prove that she was clean, he pulled
her near, against her will, and kissed her two,
three, four times. What resulted from that kissing?
One who'd just bid six hundred then withdrew.

# 6.79

Lupus, you're sad, though lucky. Don't disclose it.
    Fortune will call you thankless if she knows it.

# 6.82

Rufus, just now a man inspected me
with care, as purchasers or trainers do.
He fixed me with his eye, pointed his finger,
and said, "Aren't you the very Martial who
is known for naughty jests by all but those
who have the ear of a Batavian?"
I smiled a little smile and nodded slightly,
admitting that I was the very one.
"Then why," he asked me, "is your cloak so bad?"
"Because I'm a bad poet," I replied.
Rufus, lest this befall a poet often,
send me a better cloak to save my pride.

# 6.84

Philippus, borne by eight, is fit, but lazy.
     Avitus, if you think he's sane, you're crazy.

# 6.86

When shall I drink you, snow-cooled Setine wine,
     in plentiful cups without a doctor's ban?
Unworthy of such a boon is one who'd rather
     be heir to Midas—foolish, thankless man!
May one who hates me own vast fields of wheat,
     rivers of gold—and drink warm water, neat.

# 6.90

Gellia has one lover—that is true.
What makes it even worse: she's wife to two.

# 6.91

Our leader's sacred ban forbids adultery. You
     should be delighted, Zoilus: you don't screw.

# Book Seven

## 7.3

Why don't I send my books to you?
    For fear you'd send me *your* books, too.

## 7.4

Because his pallor, Castricus, got worse,
Oppianus started writing verse.

## 7.9

Cascellius is sixty, at his peak
    in cleverness. When will he learn to speak?

## 7.11

You make me, Pudens, emend by hand
my small books' imperfections.
You love me so—to want my trifles
with autograph corrections!

## 7.13

Dusky Lycoris went to Hercules' hills
    on hearing that old ivory turns white
in Tibur's sun. How potent Tibur's air is!
    In no time, she returned as black as night.

## 7.14

Aulus, a monstrous evil has afflicted
    my girl—she's lost her plaything and her dear:
not like the one for whom Catullus' Lesbia,
    losing her naughty sparrow, shed a tear;
nor what Ianthis mourned (and Stella sang of),
    whose black dove flies now in Elysium.
My dear's not charmed by trifles or such loves,
    nor do such losses make her heart grow glum.
She's lost a boy just twelve years old, whose dong
    was not yet fully eighteen inches long.

## 7.16

Regulus, I'm broke. All I can try
    is selling off your presents. Will you buy?

## 7.18

Since even a woman couldn't fault your face
    or flawless body, do you wonder why
a fucker rarely wants you and returns?
    Galla, you have a glaring flaw. When I
get going and we move with loins united,
    though you say nothing, your vagina's noisy.
May the gods make you speak and it be silent!
    The constant prattle of your twat annoys me.
I'd rather you farted. Symmachus says farting
    is healthy, and it makes one laugh, besides.
But who can laugh at a cunt's inane slip-slapping?
    At that, one's spirit (like one's cock) subsides.
At least speak up; drown out your raucous twat,
    or teach *it* how to talk if *you* will not.

## 7.19

What seems to you a scrap of useless wood
    was the first keel to sail the unknown sea.
What neither Clashing Rocks nor the worse wrath
    of the Black Sea could shatter formerly,
ages subdued. Though years have claimed their toll,
    the small board's more revered than the ship when whole.

## 7.21

This day, aware of a great birth, gave Lucan
    to all the people, Polla, and to you.
Harsh Nero, loathed for no death more, *this* killing,
    at least, the gods should not have let you do.

## 7.25

The epigrams you write are always bland
    and paler than skin powdered with white lead,
without a grain of wit or drop of bile,
    and still, you fool, you want them to be read!
A face without a dimple has no charm;
    food is insipid, lacking vinegar's zing.
Give honey apples and bland figs to toddlers;
    I savor Chian figs, which know how to sting.

## 7.30

You sleep with Germans, Parthians, and Dacians;
    Cilicians and Cappadocians get a screw;
a Memphian fucker sails to you from Pharos;
    a coal-black Indian from the Red Sea, too.
You don't shun pricks of circumcised Judeans;
    a Scythian on his horse won't pass you by.

Since you're a Roman girl, why is it, Caelia,
    you won't give any Roman cock a try?

# 7.39

Loath to endure and suffer more
mornings of gadding all about
and haughty greetings from great men,
Caelius started feigning gout.
Wanting too much to prove it true,
he salves and swathes his healthy feet
and walks with paces slow and pained.
How potent is his skilled deceit!
His gout is now no longer feigned.

# 7.43

Cinna, to give me what I ask is best;
    next best is to refuse without delay.
I love a giver, don't resent refusers.
    You neither give nor tell me no straightway.

# 7.46

You wish to grace your gift to me with verse
    and outdo Homer with your eloquence.
Priscus, for days you torture both of us;
    *I* suffer for your Thalia's reticence.
Send poems and ringing elegies to those
    with wealth; to poor men, give your gifts with prose.

# 7.48

Although he owns about three hundred tables,
Annius uses pageboys in their place.
The platters run right past; the dishes speed.

You fine lords, keep such banquets for yourselves:
a walking dinner puts me off my feed.

# 7.62

With doors ajar, you sodomize big youths
    and would be caught, Hamillus, doing so,
lest freedmen, family slaves, and envious clients
    gossip and carry stories. He who'd show
he *isn't* sodomized does otherwise—
    and often—when he's sure there are no spies.

# 7.70

You dyke of dykes, Philaenis, rightly you
call that girl your "girlfriend" whom you screw.

# 7.75

You want free fucks, though you're a hag and hideous.
    You want to play and not to pay? Ridiculous!

# 7.76

If powerful men—at banquets, porticoes,
and plays—compete to have you by their side;
if every time they meet you, they're delighted
to offer you a hot bath or a ride;
don't get too vain about it, Philomusus.
They love not *you*, but pleasure you provide.

# 7.77

You demand my books as gifts. I won't concede them.
    Tucca, you want to sell them, not to read them.

# 7.78

One lizardfish tail, salt-cured, Papylus,
    and oiled beans, if you're dining well, are placed
before you. You send udder, mushrooms, oysters,
    mullet, hare, boar. You've neither sense nor taste.

# 7·79

I just drank consular wine. You ask, Severus,
how old and generous it was? The wine
had been laid down when Priscus was the consul—
the very man with whom I'd come to dine.

# 7·81

"In this book, thirty poems are bad," you state.
    Lausus, if thirty are good, the book is great.

# 7·83

Circling Lupercus' face, Eutrapelus cleared
    his cheeks—while yet another beard appeared.

# 7·85

Sabellus, that you write some witty quatrains
    and craft some couplets well earns my regard,
but no surprise. To write good epigrams
    is easy, but to write a book is hard.

# 7·89

Go, lucky rose, and crown with your soft garland
my dear Appolinaris' locks—and do
not fail to bind them when they're white, years later.
For that, may Venus always cherish you.

# 7·90

Matho alleges that my book's uneven.
    He compliments my poems, if that's true.
Calvinus and Umber write consistent books.
    Consistent books are lousy through and through.

# 7·91

Eloquent Juvenal, look, I send you nuts
    for the Saturnalia, from my small plot's stock.

Its guardian god bestowed the rest of the crop
    on wanton girls, to sate his lustful cock.

# 7.92

Twice or thrice daily, Baccara, you tell me,
    "You know you needn't ask, whatever you need."
Surly Secundus duns me in harsh tones:
    you hear it, and you don't know what I need.
My rent's sought, in your presence, loud and clear:
    you hear it, and you don't know what I need.
I grumble that my cloak is worn and chilly:
    you hear it, and you don't know what I need.
Here's what I need: a star to strike you mute,
    so that you can't repeat "whatever you need."

# 7.94

Once perfume, while the onyx vial held it,
    it's fish sauce now that Papylus has smelled it.

# Book Eight

## 8.1

Book, as you enter Caesar's laureled dwelling,
    learn to speak chastely and more bashfully.
Begone, nude Venus! This book's not for you.
    May *you*, Caesar's Minerva, come to me.

## 8.5

By giving rings to girls, you lost the right,
Macer, to own the gold ring of a knight.

## 8.10

Buying a first-rate purple cloak
for ten grand, Bassus made
a profit. "Was it such a bargain?"
No—he never paid.

## 8.12

You ask why I don't want a wealthy wife?
    To be *her* wife is more than I could bear.
A wife should be below her husband, Priscus,
    for man and wife to be a well-matched pair.

## 8.13

Gargilianus, return my cash! I bought
    your so-called fool for twenty grand. He's not.

# 8.14

So your Cilician fruit trees won't turn pale
    in fear of winter, nor harsh breezes bite
your tender grove, glass panes block cold south winds,
    admitting clear sun and unsullied light.
*I* get a room whose window's stuck ajar,
    where Boreas himself could get no rest.
You'd have an old friend lodge like this, you brute?
    I'd be more sheltered as your orchard's guest.

# 8.16

You were a baker long before;
Cyperus, you're a lawyer now.
Each year you earn two hundred thou,
but spend it all and borrow more.
You're still a baker now, although
you're making flour out of dough.

# 8.17

I pled your case for two grand, as agreed,
    so, Sextus, what's this paltry thousand for?
"You didn't state the facts, and you lost the case."
    I blushed, though, so for *that* you owe me more.

# 8.18

Cerrinius, if your epigrams were published,
    you'd be my peer or even better known.
Yet such is your respect for an old friend,
    you cherish my renown beyond your own.
So Vergil did not try the odes of Horace,
    though in Pindaric measures he'd have shone;
he yielded fame for tragedy to Varius,

though *he* could better voice the tragic tone.
A friend will often give gold, wealth, and ground;
   one who will yield in talent's rarely found.

## 8.19

Cinna, who makes a show of poverty,
is just as poor as he pretends to be.

## 8.20

You write two hundred lines a day, but don't recite.
   Varus, you are wise, if none too bright.

## 8.22

You invite me for boar, but pork is what I'm fed.
   I'm a hybrid, Gallicus, if I'm misled.

## 8.23

Because I beat my cook for spoiling dinner,
   you think I'm picky, Rusticus, and rash.
If *that* seems insufficient cause for whipping,
   for what, then, *does* a cook deserve the lash?

## 8.25

When I was quite ill, you called just once on me.
I'll visit, Oppianus, frequently.

## 8.27

Gaurus, you're old and rich. Those who stop by
   with gifts (could you but know) are saying "Die."

## 8.29

A couplet writer tries to please by terseness.
   What good is brevity in a *book* of verses?

# 8.31

Dento, when you, who have a wife, petition
    for rights reserved for men who've fathered three,
you're making an unsavory admission.
    Go home. Stop tiring Caesar with your plea.
While searching, long and far from the wife you spurn,
    for *three* kids, you'll find *four* on your return.

# 8.35

You lead such matching, equal lives—
the worst of husbands, worst of wives—
that it's a mystery to me
why you aren't suited perfectly.

# 8.40

Priapus, you guard not plots or vines,
but the sparse grove where you were born
and can be born again. Keep out
thieves' hands and save the copse, I warn,
for its master's fireplace: if it should
run short, you too are made of wood.

# 8.41

"Downhearted, Athenagoras hasn't sent us
    midwinter gifts as usual." I'll see
whether *he*'s gloomy later on, Faustinus.
    One thing is certain: he has saddened *me*.

# 8.43

Chrestilla buries husbands; Fabius, wives.
    Each waves the funeral torch at the marriage bed.

Pair up the winners, Venus. The result
    will be that both will share a bier instead.

# 8.47

Part of your jaws is clipped, part shaved instead,
    part plucked. Who'd think it's all a single head?

# 8.51

Though Asper's love, no doubt, is shaped to please,
    he's blind. He loves, in truth, more than he sees.

# 8.54

Loveliest of all girls who were or are,
of all who were or are, you're most debased.
Catulla, how I wish you would become
less beautiful or—failing that—more chaste.

# 8.56

You often give great gifts and will give greater,
    outdoing yourself and other leaders, too,
but people don't adore you for your bounty:
    Caesar, they love your gifts because of you.

# 8.60

You'd match Nero's Colossus if you might
    take eighteen inches, Claudia, from your height.

# 8.61

Charinus turns green with envy, bursts, fumes, cries,
and seeks to hang himself from a high bough,
not that I'm read throughout the world, nor that,
adorned with bosses and cedar oil, I'm now
spread through all nations Rome controls, but that

I own a rural summer home near town
and ride *my* mules, not rented ones, today.
What curse on him, Severus, should I call down?
May *he* own mules and a place near town, I pray.

# 8.62

Though Picens writes verses on backs of sheets, it galls him
    that Phoebus turns his back while Picens scrawls them.

# 8.69

Vacerra, you admire the ancients only
and praise no poets but those here no more.
I beg that you will pardon me, Vacerra,
but pleasing you is not worth dying for.

# 8.76

"Tell me the truth, please, Marcus," you implore.
"Nothing could be more welcome to my ear."
Whenever you recite your books or plead
a client's case, you'd have me be sincere.
It's hard for me to turn down your request.
So, Gallicus, hear this truth, loud and clear:
the truth is not what you desire to hear.

# 8.77

Liber, beloved by friends, worthy of living
    crowned with eternal roses, if you're clever,
let your hair glisten with Assyrian scent
    and floral garlands deck your head forever.
Let old Falernian darken your clear crystal,
    a charming lover warm your downy bed.
Who's lived thus, though he die in middle age,
    has stretched his life beyond its granted thread.

# 8.79

All of your friends are ancient hags
or eyesores uglier than those.
These are the company you drag
to banquets, plays, and porticoes.
Fabulla, when you're seen among
such friends, you're beautiful and young.

# Book Nine

## 9.4

Since Galla can be fucked for two gold coins,
    and sodomized for merely twice that sum,
why, Aeschylus, does she get *ten* from you?
    She sucks for less. For what, then? Staying mum.

## 9.6

Since your return from Libya, five days straight
    I sought to greet you, Afer. On each try,
I'm told "He's busy," "He's asleep." Enough!
    You don't want greetings, Afer? Then goodbye.

## 9.8

Fabius, whom you gave six grand a year,
    has left you nothing. He left no one more.
Bithynicus, don't grumble. He has left you
    six grand a year more than you had before.

## 9.9

Though, Cantharus, you're fond of dining out,
you hurl abuse, you threaten, and you shout.
I warn you, leave your truculence behind:
you can't both stuff your face and speak your mind.

## 9.10

You'd like to wed Priscus, Paula? That's no surprise:
    you're wise. He'd rather not. He too is wise.

## 9.14

You think this fellow has a friend's true heart,
    who likes you for your spread and how you dine?
He loves sow's udder, mullet, boar, and oysters.
    If I dined so, he'd be a friend of mine.

## 9.15

On seven husbands' tombs, Chloe the murderess
    wrote "Chloe's work." What more could she confess?

## 9.19

You praise, Sabellus, in three hundred verses,
the baths of Ponticus, whose dinners shine.
You do not want to bathe; you want to dine.

## 9.21

Artemidorus sold his field to buy a boy,
    whom Calliodorus sold to get the field.
Artemidorus plays and Calliodorus plows.
    Which of them, Auctus, gets a better yield?

## 9.25

Whenever we watch your Hyllus serving wine,
    you fix us, Afer, with a troubled eye.
What crime is it to look at a soft page?
    We view the sun, stars, temples, gods. Should I
avert my gaze as if a Gorgon offered
    the cup, hiding my eyes and face? Indeed,

though Hercules was fierce, one could view Hylas;
    Mercury can play with Ganymede.
If guests can't watch your young boys serving wine,
    ask Oedipuses and Phineuses to dine.

## 9.32

I want an easy girl, who roams in a cloak,
    who puts out for my slave ahead of me,
who sells for two denarii all she has,
    who simultaneously can service three.
She who talks big and asks large sums may go
    oblige the cock of a blockhead from Bordeaux.

## 9.33

Flaccus, when at the baths you hear applause,
I'm certain Maro's cock must be the cause.

## 9.40

When Diodorus left for Rome from Pharos
to seek the Tarpeian wreath, Philaenis swore
(naive girl!) that on his return she'd lick
what even modest Sabine wives adore.
His ship broke up in a raging storm, and though
waves swamped him and he foundered in the sea,
he still swam back to shore to claim her pledge.
What a slow husband! What great lethargy!
Had *my* girl, on the shore, made such a vow,
I'd have returned with her immediately.

## 9.44

I just asked Vindex whose fine work
his sculpture of Alcides was.
"Poet, don't you know Greek?" he asked
with a laugh and nod, the way he does.
"The name's inscribed on the base." I read
"Lysippus"; Phidias, *I'd* have said.

# 9.50

Gaurus, you claim that since my poems please
    by brevity, my talent's second rate.
I grant they're short. But you who write twelve books
    on Priam's mighty battles, are you great?
I make small boys of bronze, who live and play;
    you, great one, make a giant out of clay.

# 9.52

Believe me, Quintus Ovidius, I love
your birthday, April first, as much as mine,
March first—for you deserve it. Both are blessed,
days marked with choicer pebbles as a sign.
One gave me life; the other, a best friend.
Yours, Quintus, gives me more joy, in the end.

# 9.53

I wished to give a trifling birthday gift,
    Quintus, which you forbid imperiously.
I must obey. Let's do what both would wish,
    what pleases both. Let *you* give one to *me*.

# 9.60

Whether you come from Paestum's fields or Tibur's,
    whether your blooms made Tusculan soil blush red,
adorned Campania lately, or were plucked
    by a steward's wife from a Praenestine bed,
let my Sabinus (to lend your wreath more charm)
    assume you've come from my Nomentan farm.

# 9.62

Philaenis is arrayed in purple
every day (and evenings, too),
but isn't showy or stuck-up:
she likes their odor, not their hue.

# 9.63

You're asked to dinner, Phoebus, by every queen.
    I'd say one fed by a cock is none too clean.

# 9.66

Your wife is lovely, chaste, and young, Fabullus,
    so why beg Caesar for a father's perks?
What you beseech our lord and god to grant you,
    you'll give yourself, if your equipment works.

# 9.67

All night I had a randy girl, whose mischief
    none can exhaust. Worn out from having tried
a thousand modes, I asked her for the boy way.
    Before I'd started begging, she complied.
Laughing and blushing, I asked for something ruder.
    At once the wanton girl gave her permission.
To me, she's pure still; Aeschylus, she *won't* be
    to you—if you accept her lewd condition.

# 9.69

You tend to shit at the climax of a screw.
    When buggered, Polycharmus, what do you do?

# 9.74

A painting shows Camonius as a boy;
    in this alone, the child's small form lives on.
No portrait from his prime was made, his father
    fearing to see his face with all speech gone.

# 9.78

Galla had buried seven husbands, Picentinus; then
    she married you. Galla, I think, would like to join her men.

# 9.80

A starving pauper wed a wealthy crone.
    Gellius feeds his wife and gives her the bone.

# 9.81

Though listener and reader like my books,
    some poet, Aulus, says they lack finesse.
I don't much care. I'd far rather impress
    the diners with my courses than the cooks.

# 9.82

An astrologer said that shortly you'd be doomed,
    nor do I reckon, Munna, that he lied.
You drained your family wealth through lavish spending
    for fear of leaving something when you died.
In less than a year, two million was consumed:
    Tell me, is this not shortly to be doomed?

# 9.83

For all the feats of your arena, Caesar,
    which beat the famous shows of former leaders,
our eyes confess great debt, our ears still more,
    for you've made watchers of habitual readers.

# 9.85

Atilius, when Paulus feels unwell,
    his dinner guests must fast—but not the host.
Your sudden illness, Paulus, is fictitious,
    but my free meal has given up the ghost.

# 9.87

When, after seven cups of wine,
I'm fuddled and my speech is slurred,

you bring who-knows-what document,
saying, "I've recently conferred
freedom on Nasta, Father's slave.
Seal here." Not now, Lupercus. Ask
tomorrow: that's more suitable.
For now, my ring seals just the flask.

## 9.88

Rufus, when you pursued me, you'd send presents;
    now that I'm caught, you give me none at all.
To keep your captive, go on sending gifts,
    or else the ill-fed boar may flee the stall.

## 9.89

Stella, your rule's too hard, that guests must versify!
    "You may, of course, write *bad* verse," you reply.

## 9.91

If Caesar's messenger and Jove's should call me
    to dine in different heavens, though the sky
were closer and the Palace farther off,
    I'd send this answer to the gods on high:
"Search on for one who'd be Jove's company;
    *my* Jupiter keeps me on earth, you see."

## 9.96

Doctor Herodes took a patient's scoop for wine by stealth.
    When caught, he said, "You nitwit, drinking's ruining your
        health."

## 9.100

For three denarii, you bid me come
    to pay you morning calls in formal dress,
then stay beside you, walk before your litter,
    and call upon ten widows, more or less.

My toga may be threadbare, cheap, and graying,
  but, Bassus, it costs more than you are paying.

## 9.102

You cancel the four hundred grand I owe you.
  Give me instead a hundred grand in loan.
Boast of your useless gift to others, Phoebus:
  what I can't pay you, I *already* own.

# Book Ten

## 10.1

If as a book I seem too long, my end
    too far, to make me short, read just a few.
My short page often ends at a poem's end,
    so make me just as brief as pleases you.

## 10.8

Paula would marry me; I'm disinclined.
    She's old. If she were older, I'd change my mind.

## 10.9

I, Martial, am renowned for poetry
of eleven feet or syllables, acclaimed
for ample wit, without effrontery,
by tribes and nations—but why envy me?
The horse Andraemon is as widely famed.

## 10.16

Aper shot his wealthy wife—an arrow through her heart
    during a game of archery. At gamesmanship, he's smart.

## 10.21

Sextus, why relish writing what Claranus
    and skilled Modestus barely comprehend?

Your books need not a reader, but Apollo.
Cinna outrivaled Vergil, you contend.
Let *your* verse earn such praise; let *my* creations
please scholars without needing explications.

## 10.22

You ask why I paint healthy lips
with white lead and my chin with goo
often when I go out, Philaenis?
I'm not fond of kissing you.

## 10.23

Happy Antonius Primus now has numbered
fifteen Olympiads of tranquil years.
He looks back on past days and years securely,
not dreading Lethe's water as it nears.
No day that he recalls is grim or painful;
there's none whose memory he would avoid.
A good man can expand his life: he lives
twice over whose past life can be enjoyed.

## 10.27

The senate on your birthday, Diodorus,
reclines as guests of yours; few knights are missed.
Your dole is lavish: thirty coins apiece.
Yet no one is aware that you exist.

## 10.29

The dish you used to send at the Saturnalia,
you sent your mistress; the green dinner gown
you gave her on the first of March was purchased
instead of buying *me* a toga. Now,
Sextilianus, you get girls for free:
you fuck them with the gifts you once gave me.

## 10.31

You lately sold a servant for twelve hundred
    to dine well, Calliodorus, just one time.
But you did *not* dine well: the four-pound mullet
    you bought as the meal's showpiece was a crime.
One wants to shout, "That's not a fish, you beast!
    That's no fish! That's a man on whom you feast."

## 10.32

You ask, Caedicianus, whom this picture,
    adorned with roses and violets, portrays?
That's Marcus Antonius Primus in midlife.
    In this the old man views his younger face.
If only art could show his heart and spirit!
    For loveliness, no painting could come near it.

## 10.39

You swear you were born when Brutus led us. Liar!
    Lesbia, were you born in Numa's day?
There, too, you lie: those who recount your eons
    report Prometheus molded you from clay.

## 10.40

My Polla, I was always told,
saw a queer friend a lot
in private. Lupus, I broke in.
A faggot he was not.

## 10.43

You've buried seven wives now in your field.
    Phileros, no one's land can top *that* yield.

## 10.44

To visit, Quintus Ovidius, Caledonians,
    green Tethys and Father Ocean, do you yield

the hills of Numa and Nomentan leisure,
    parted in old age from your hearth and field?
You postpone joys, but Atropos keeps spinning,
    and every hour's added to your sum.
You will have shown your friend (who wouldn't praise it?)
    that keeping your word means more than life. But come
back to your Sabine home at last to dwell,
    counting *yourself* among your friends as well.

## 10.45

If my small books say something smooth and sweet,
    if a suave page sounds flattering, you deplore
such greasy fare; you'd rather gnaw a rib
    when I serve loin of a Laurentian boar.
My flask's not to your taste: drink Vatican
    if vinegar delights your palate more.

## 10.47

Most genial Martial, these things are
the elements that make life blessed:
money inherited, not earned;
a fire year-round, a mind at rest,
productive land, no lawsuits, togas
rarely, friends of like degree,
a gentleman's physique, sound health,
shrewd innocence, good company,
plain fare, nights carefree, yet not drunk;
a bed that's decent, not austere;
sleep, to make darkness brief; desire
to be just what you are, no higher;
and death no cause for hope or fear.

## 10.49

Though you drink drafts of amethyst
and swill Opimian, dark and old,
you toast me in new Sabine wine.

"Would you prefer it served in gold?"
you ask me. Cotta, who would sup
leaden wine from a golden cup?

## 10.52

Numa saw Thelys the eunuch in formal dress
and called him a condemned adulteress.

## 10.53

I'm Scorpus, the glory of the roaring Circus,
　　Rome's short-lived darling, cheered for a brief span,
then seized by jealous Fate at twenty-seven.
　　Counting my wins, she thought me an old man.

## 10.54

You cover your fine tables. Get a clue!
　　Olus, like *that*, I own fine tables, too.

## 10.59

If just one poem fills a page, you skip it.
　　The short ones please you, not the best. I serve
a lavish dinner culled from every market,
　　but you are only pleased with the hors d'oeuvre.
A finicky reader's not for me; instead,
　　I want one who's not full without some bread.

## 10.61

Here rests Erotion's all-too-hurried shade,
　　dispatched in her sixth winter by Fate's crime.
Make yearly offerings to her tiny ghost,
　　whoever rules this plot after my time.
So may your home and household last for years
　　with nothing but this stone to call for tears.

# 10.64

Polla, my queen, if you take up my books,
    receive my jests without a frown of scorn.
Your bard, the glory of our Helicon,
    who blew fierce war on his Pierian horn,
in bawdy verses didn't blush to say,
    "Cotta, if I'm not sodomized, why stay?"

# 10.65

Since *you* boast you're a citizen of Corinth,
Charmenion, which no one can deny,
why call me "brother," when I come from Tagus,
born of Iberians and Celts. Do I
look similar to you? You roam resplendent
with curled locks; I have stubborn Spanish hair.
You're smooth from daily depilation; I
have shins and cheeks with bristles everywhere.
Your mouth lisps and your tongue is weak, but only
Silia's voice is more robust than mine.
A dove is not more different from an eagle,
a shy gazelle from an unyielding lion.
So cease to call me "brother" so that I
don't start to call you "sister" in reply.

# 10.66

Who, Theopompus, bid you be a cook?
    Who was so proud, so heartless? Could one bear
to desecrate this face with kitchen soot
    or let a greasy fire pollute this hair?
Whose hand can better hold wine-scoops and crystal,
    or, mixing it, improve Falernian's taste?

Let Jupiter make Ganymede his cook
    if starlike pages thus can go to waste.

## 10.74

Rome, spare at last the tired congratulator,
the weary client. How long shall I call
among the escorts and the men in togas,
earning a hundred cents a day in all,
while Scorpus for one hour's win takes home
fifteen full bags of new gold coin in gains?
I wouldn't want my books to be rewarded—
for what are *they* worth?—with Apulian plains.
Not Hybla nor the grain-rich Nile attracts me,
nor the delightful grape that from the steep
summit of Setia's slope views Pomptine marshes.
What do I want, you ask? I want to sleep.

## 10.77

Maximus, nothing Carus did was naughtier
    than dying of fever. It, too, was unfair!
Harsh, heinous fever, if you'd just been milder!
    He should have been saved—for his physician's care.

## 10.80

Eros weeps when viewing murrine cups
    or boys or tables made of citrus wood.
He groans that he can't buy the whole Enclosure.
    He'd take it home, poor fellow, if he could.
How many do like Eros, but dry-eyed!
    Most ridicule his tears—and weep inside.

## 10.81

When two arrived one morning to fuck Phyllis,
    each longed to take her naked first. To meet
their wish, she vowed she'd service both at once—
    and did: one raised her tunic; one, her feet.

## 10.84

You wonder why Afer doesn't go to bed?
    You see who lies beside him. Enough said.

## 10.90

Why pluck your ancient cunt, Ligeia,
stirring up buried ash and bone?
Such daintiness suits girls, but you
no longer can be called a crone.
Trust me, it's nice for Hector's wife,
but for his mother it's unfit.
You're wrong to think you have a cunt
now that a cock's unknown to it.
Ligeia, show some shame at least:
don't pluck its beard when the lion's deceased.

## 10.91

Almo owns only eunuchs, his cock is no use,
    yet he gripes that Polla fails to reproduce.

## 10.94

No serpent of Numidia guards my orchard,
    nor does Alcinous' royal land serve me.
My farm's Nomentan trees bear fruit in safety;
    their leaden apples fear no thievery.
I therefore send these yellow fruits of autumn,
    produced in mid-Subura recently.

## 10.95

Your spouse and lover returned your brat to you,
    denying they fucked you, Galla. What *did* you do?

## 10.97

As a pyre was built with flammable papyrus,
    the weeping wife bought myrrh and spice to strew.

When undertaker, bier, and grave were ready,
    Numa named me his heir—and then pulled through.

## 10.100

You fool, why mix your verse with mine? A book
at odds with itself, poor man, does you no good.
Why try to herd your foxes with the lions
and make owls look like eagles? Even should
you have one foot as swift as Ladas, blockhead,
you can't run if the other leg is wood.

## 10.102

How did Philinus, you inquire,
who never fucks, become a sire?
Ask Gaditanus, if you'd know it,
who never writes, though he's a poet.

# Book Eleven

## 11.13

Don't pass this famous marble by
while walking the Flaminian Way.
Rome's darling and the wit of Nile,
talent and grace, delight and play,
the grief and glory of Rome's stage,
and all the love gods met their doom,
buried with Paris in this tomb.

## 11.14

Don't bury the little farmer, heirs, for soil,
    however light, to him means heavy toil.

## 11.15

I've pages Cato's wife might read,
and Sabine wives of daunting looks,
but I want this whole book to laugh,
outdoing all the bawdy books.
Let it be wine-soaked and not blush
at stains from Cosmus' rich pomade,
play with the boys and love the girls,
naming outright the part that made
us all, our common parent, which
virtuous Numa called his cock.
Recall, Apollinaris, these

are Saturnalian verses. Please
    don't judge my morals by this book.

## 11.17

Sabinus, not all of my pages suit the night.
    You'll find some you can read by morning light.

## 11.19

Why won't I wed you, Galla? You're well-read.
    My cock makes frequent grammar slips in bed.

## 11.25

That randy cock of Linus, known among
    a host of girls, won't stand. So watch out, tongue.

## 11.28

At Doctor Euctus' house, mad Nasica attacked
    and buggered his Hylas. I'd say his wit's intact.

## 11.29

When your old hand starts stroking my limp cock,
    Phyllis, I'm murdered by your thumb, and when
you call me "mouse" or "light of my eyes," I think
    ten hours will hardly rally me again.
You don't know coaxing. Say "I'll give you acres
    of fruitful Setine soil and a hundred grand.
Take wine, a house, boys, gold-trimmed plates, and tables."
    *That's* how to rub me. Then you'll need no hand.

## 11.30

You say the mouths of lawyers and writers of verse
    smell bad. But, Zoilus, mouths that suck smell worse.

## 11.34

Aper bought a dark and ancient cottage,
    in which not even an owl would wish to dwell.

But Maro owns a fine estate nearby.
    Aper will live in poor style, but dine well.

## 11.35

You ask three hundred people I don't know
and then you act astonished, fume, and moan
because I won't come too when I'm invited.
Fabullus, I don't like to dine alone.

## 11.37

Why, Zoilus, do you waste that poor sardonyx,
    surrounding it with one whole pound of setting?
Lately, a ring like that would link your shins.
    The same weight on a finger isn't fitting.

## 11.38

Someone paid twenty grand for a muleteer.
    Does the price surprise you, Aulus? He couldn't hear.

## 11.40

Lupercus loves fair Glycera;
he is her only lord and owner.
He griped to Aelianus that
for one whole month he couldn't bone her.
Asked what he was waiting for,
he answered that her teeth were sore.

## 11.42

You call for lively verse—on lifeless themes.
    But how, Caecilianus? You decree
you'll have Hyblaean or Hymettian honey,
    yet offer Corsican thyme to the Attic bee.

## 11.43

Catching me with a boy, you scold me, wife.
    and say you have an asshole, too. Agreed!

So Juno often said to lustful Jove,
     yet still he lies with strapping Ganymede.
Hercules dropped his bow and bent his Hylas.
     Do you think Megara lacked an ass? Denied
his fleeing Daphne, Phoebus was tormented,
     but Hyacinthus made those flames subside.
Briseis often turned her back to Achilles,
     yet his smooth friend was nearer. Don't allot
masculine names to your belongings, wife:
     just think that you possess a second twat.

## 11.44

You're childless, rich, and born when Brutus led us.
     Do you believe your friendships to be true?
Some are—the ones you had when young and poor.
     Your new friends would be glad to bury you.

## 11.45

Each time you cross a labeled bedroom's threshold,
     whether a boy or girl has caught your eye,
you're not content with curtains, doors, and bolts;
     you want more privacy, so none can spy.
If there's suspicion of the slightest chink
     or holes bored by a lewd pin, they're caulked, too.
Nobody is so worried or so modest
     who wants to bugger, Cantharus, or screw.

## 11.46

Mevius, you don't rise, except in sleep;
     your cock starts pissing on your feet instead.
Your shriveled dick is pressed by weary fingers,

  but, urged thus, doesn't lift its lifeless head.
Why pester cunts and butts in vain? To thrive,
    go high up: that's where old cocks come alive.

# 11.47

So why does Lattara shun all baths beloved
    by female hordes? He doesn't want to fuck.
Why won't he stroll in Pompey's shade or visit
    Isis' shrine? He doesn't want to fuck.
Why pour cold water on his body, smeared
    with Spartan mud? He doesn't want to fuck.
Since he shuns womankind thus, why does Lattara
    lick a cunt? He doesn't want to fuck.

# 11.50

Till now, only a pauper honored Vergil's
    neglected tomb and hallowed memory.
Silius chose to help his slighted shade,
    and honors the poet, no less poet he.

# 11.51

From Titius hangs a column as immense
as that the girls of Lampsacus revere.
He bathes in spacious bathtubs of his own
with none to jostle him or crowd too near.
And yet he's cramped for room, bathing alone.

# 11.57

Severus, do you wonder that I send you,
    a poet, verse when asking you to dine?
Jove has his fill of nectar and ambrosia,

yet still we offer him raw guts and wine.
　　The gods gave you all gifts. With such a lot,
　　　　what can I give you that you haven't got?

## 11.60

Is Chione or Phlogis better in bed?
　　　　Chione's fairer; Phlogis is on fire.
Phlogis could tauten Priam's floppy strap
　　　　or make old Pelias young with her desire.
She has the itch one wants one's girl to have,
　　　　which Criton, not Hygia, can allay.
But Chione feels nothing, makes no sound:
　　　　you'd think she'd turned to stone or gone away.
You gods, if one might win so much from you,
　　　　if you would offer benefits so rich,
may you give Chione's physique to Phlogis
　　　　while letting Chione have Phlogis' itch.

## 11.62

Lesbia swears she never gives free lays.
　　　　It's true: when she gets fucked, she always pays.

## 11.63

Watching me while I bathe, you often comment
that my smooth boys are well endowed—how come?
I'll give you a frank answer, Philomusus:
they bugger busybodies in the bum.

## 11.64

I don't know what you write to all those girls; I do
　　　　know *this* much, Faustus: no girl writes to you.

## 11.66

You're an informer, slanderer,
cocksucker, swindler, panderer,
and fight instructor. It seems funny,
Vacerra, that you have no money.

# 11.67

Alive, you give me nothing, saying you'll bequeath me more.
    Maro, if you're no fool, you know what *I* am hoping for.

# 11.68

Though you ask great men for small things, you're denied.
    Ask big things, Matho, to preserve your pride.

# 11.71

To her old husband Leda claimed hysteria;
    fucking, for her, she wails, is a true *need*,
but she denies, with tears and moans, that living
    is worth the price; she'd rather die, indeed.
He begs her to live and not give up her prime.
    What he can't do is done by his decree.
The female doctors leave; the male ones come.
    Her feet are lifted. Drastic remedy!

# 11.72

Natta calls his athlete's cock his "weenie"—
    compared to *it*, Priapus would look teeny.

# 11.75

Your slave bathes with you, Caelia,
encased in a bronze sheath. But why,
since he's no singer to the lyre
or flute? I guess so you won't spy
his cock. So why bathe publicly?
Are we all eunuchs, then, to you?
Not to seem grudging, therefore, take
the cock-shield off your servant, too.

# 11.76

Paetus, you make me pay you back ten thousand,
    since Bucco lost two hundred thousand. When

the sins aren't mine, I beg, don't let them harm me.
    You, who can lose two hundred grand, lose ten.

## 11.77

For hours all day Vacerra sits
in all the privies. Constipation?
No, he doesn't want to shit;
he wants a dinner invitation.

## 11.79

Because I came an hour late for dinner,
    I'm charged with being indolent and slow.
Paetus, the fault's not mine and not the road's—
    it's yours, for sending mules that wouldn't go.

## 11.81

An old man and a eunuch, Dindymus, pester
    Aegle, a girl who lies between them dry.
One foiled by lack of strength and one by age,
    each burns with fruitless lust through every try.
Venus, she begs you'll help the luckless three:
    give one his youth and one virility.

## 11.83

You lodge none but the childless rich for free.
    No rent, Sosibianus, tops *your* fee.

## 11.85

Zoilus, while you licked, your tongue was struck
    with sudden torpor. Surely, now you fuck.

## 11.86

To soothe your sore throat, constantly inflamed
    by a harsh cough, the doctor would insist
that you get honey, nuts, sweet cakes, whatever

makes boys less fretful. Yet you still persist
in all-day coughing. This is no cough, I see;
    Parthenopaeus, this is gluttony.

# 11.87

Once you were rich; back then, you were a bugger.
    For ages, women were unknown to you.
Now you run after crones. How want compels one!
    It's even, Charidemus, made you screw.

# 11.88

Carisianus says for many days now
he couldn't sodomize. Urged to confide
the reason lately, Lupus, to his friends,
"I'm plagued with diarrhea," he replied.

# 11.89

Why send me pristine wreaths? I'd rather wear
    the rumpled roses, Polla, from your hair.

# 11.92

Whoever calls you "vicious," Zoilus, lies.
    You're not a vicious person; you're pure vice.

# 11.93

Flames took the home of poet Theodorus.
    Are the Muses and Phoebus pleased with this disaster?
What a great crime and insult to the gods
    not to have burned together home and master!

# 11.96

German, the Marcian leaps here, not the Rhine.
    Why block a boy from the ample fountain's spray?
The victors' stream should not ease captive thirst,
    barbarian, while a town slave's pushed away.

## 11.97

Four times a night I manage, Telesilla—but with you,
    damn me if once in four years isn't more than I can do.

## 11.99

When rising from your chair, I've often noticed,
    you're buggered, Lesbia, by your wretched dress.
You tug with your right and left hand till you free it,
    blubbering and moaning with distress.
It's held so by your asshole's Clashing Rocks
    as it enters where your massive buttocks meet.
Would you correct this ugly fault? Here's how:
    neither stand up, I'd say, nor take a seat.

## 11.101

Flaccus, could you see Thais, who's so spare?
    I think that you can see what isn't there.

## 11.102

Lydia, he who said your flesh was lovely,
    but not your face, did not distort the facts.
You *would* look good if you'd shut up and lie
    mute as a painting or a bust in wax.
But when you speak, you spoil your flesh, as well.
    No tongue can do itself more injury.
Make sure the aedile doesn't see and hear you:
    a talking statue is a prodigy.

## 11.103

Your mind and face, Safronius, are so mild
    I marvel that you could beget a child.

## 11.105

You used to send a pound; now it's decreased
    to a quarter, Garricus. Pay me half, at least.

## 11.106

If, Vibius Maximus, you've time for greetings,
read just this; you're too occupied to view
them all and none too fond of what takes effort.
You've skipped these four lines, also? Wise of you.

## 11.108

Reader, so long a book should satisfy you,
    yet still "a few more couplets," you reply.
But boys want food and Lupus wants his interest.
    Pay up! You're silent, playing deaf? Goodbye.

# Book Twelve

### 12.7

If she has just as many years, all told,
as hairs on her head, Ligeia's three years old.

### 12.9

Most gentle Caesar, Palma rules our Spaniards,
    and Peace abroad enjoys his mild command.
We gladly thank you for so great a gift:
    you've sent your own good nature to our land.

### 12.10

Although worth millions, Africanus hunts a legacy.
To many, Fortune gives too much, enough to nobody.

### 12.12

When you've drunk all night, you promise all things, but bestow
    nothing next day. Drink early, Pollio.

### 12.13

The rich believe it pays to get irate—
to give is costlier, Auctus, than to hate.

### 12.16

You sold three little fields
to buy three slave boys; now

you still have, Labienus,
three little fields to plow.

## 12.17

You often groan, Laetinus, and ask why
    your fever stays so many days with you.
It rides your litter, bathes with you, and dines
    on mushrooms, oysters, boar, and udder, too.
It's often drunk on Setine or Falernian,
    quaffs only Caecuban that snow has chilled.
It lies enwreathed in roses, dark with unguents,
    and sleeps on purple couches, feather filled.
Living so well with you, so cosseted,
    why would it move to Dama's house instead?

## 12.18

While you, perhaps, roam loud Subura, restless,
or trudge Diana's hill, your sweaty gown
fanning you through the thresholds of the mighty,
Juvenal, a wanderer worn down
by the greater and the lesser Caelian hills,
my Bilbilis, which vaunts her iron and gold,
returned to after numerous Decembers,
received me, now a rustic, to her fold.
Here, idle, I take pleasant pains to visit
Boterdus and Platea (so bizarre
are names in Celtiberian lands), and revel
in huge, unseemly bouts of sleep, which are
often unbroken well past nine or ten,
paying myself back fully now at last
for thirty years of vigils. Togas now
are quite unknown, but when I ask, I'm passed
the nearest garment from a broken chair.
Rising, I'm welcomed by a hearth with lots
of splendid logs from nearby oak-woods, crowned

by the steward's wife with hordes of cooking pots.
The huntsman follows, but the sort you'd wish
to have beside you in a hidden wood.
My smooth-skinned steward gives my boys their food
and begs to cut his long hair. Truly I
rejoice to live like this, like this to die.

### 12.20

Themison has no wife—and never missed her.
Fabullus, you ask why? He has a sister.

### 12.22

In few words, just how ugly is
one-eyed Philaenis? To my mind,
Fabullus, she'd look better blind.

### 12.23

You use bought teeth and hair without a thought.
    But, Laelia, an eye? That can't be bought.

### 12.26

The bandits fucked you, Saenia, so you say;
however, all the bandits say "No way!"

### 12.27

While *I* drink two drafts, you drink two—plus nine.
    And you grumble, Cinna, that we drink different wine?

### 12.30

So what if Aper's sober! I commend
abstinence in a slave, not in a friend.

### 12.31

This grove, these springs, this arbor of laced vines,
    this channeled flowing stream, the grassy fields;

fresh vegetables, not nipped by January;
  rose beds that equal Paestum's twofold yields;
the household eel that swims in fenced-in waters;
  the whitewashed turret holding birds as white—
these are my lady's gifts. Marcella gave
  this house, this little realm, to me outright
when, after thirty-five years, I came home.
  If offered her father's gardens by Nausicaa,
I'd tell Alcinous, "I prefer my own."

## 12.34

The summers, Julius, that we've shared,
if I recall, were thirty-four.
Their sweets were mixed with bitters, yet
still the delightful times were more.
If pebbles marking good and bad
were piled in two heaps, here and there,
the white ones would surpass the black.
To shield your heart from biting care
and shun some kinds of bitterness,
don't grow too close to any friend:
your joy and grief will both be less.

## 12.35

You often tell me you've been sodomized,
  Callistratus, as if you know me well.
You're not as candid as you wish to seem.
  Who tells such things has more he *doesn't* tell.

## 12.40

You lie and I believe it. You recite bad verse: I praise it.
  You sing: I sing. You drink: I drink. You fart and I play
    dumb.
I lose to you, Pontilianus, each time we play checkers.
  You do one thing without me—on that subject, I stay mum.

For me you don't do anything. "But once I'm dead," you say,
    "I'll treat you well." I don't want anything—but die today.

## 12.42

Bearded Callistratus wed rugged Afer
    the way a virgin usually is mated.
The torches shone, his face was veiled in orange,
    the ritual words were cried, the dowry stated.
Rome, is this *still* unsatisfactory? Maybe
    you're waiting for the bride to have a baby?

## 12.45

With kidskin you conceal your bare
temples and pate, in place of hair.
How witty was the man who said,
Phoebus, you have a well-shod head.

## 12.46

You're difficult and easy, sweet and tart.
    I cannot live with you, nor live apart.

## 12.47

Lupercus and Gallus sell their verse for gain.
Now, Classicus, say *poets* are insane!

## 12.51

Why's Fabullinus easy to deceive?
A good man, Aulus, always is naïve.

## 12.56

Ten times or more a year you're taken ill,
    but, Polycharmus, *we're* the ones who suffer.
Each time you rise, you ask your friends for presents.
    For shame! This time get sick and don't recover.

## 12.58

Your wife says you like slave girls; she's attached
    to litter-men. Alauda, you're well matched.

## 12.61

You fear I'll write a brief and lively poem
attacking you, Ligurra, and you yearn
to seem one who would merit such a fear.
Your wish is vain and so is your concern.
Lions of Libya roar at bulls; they leave
butterflies unmolested. If you're keen
to have men read of you, find some drunk bard
of the dark arch, who scrawls on a latrine,
in clumsy charcoal or in crumbling chalk,
verses that people read while they are shitting.
To mark your brow with *my* brand isn't fitting.

## 12.64

One finer in face and hair than rosy pageboys, Cinna placed
    among his cooks. Cinna is such a glutton in his taste!

## 12.65

Fair Phyllis had obliged me all night long,
amply, in every manner. As I bent
my mind next morning on what gift to give her—
a pound of Niceros' or Cosmus' scent,
great weights of Spanish wool, or ten gold coins
from Caesar's mint—she pressed her lips to mine
in a long, coaxing kiss, like courting doves,
and started asking for a jar of wine.

## 12.69

Just like your pictures and drinking cups, to you,
    Paulus, your friends are all authentic, too.

## 12.71

Nothing I ask for, Lygdus, you provide,
but formerly there's nothing you denied.

## 12.73

You say I am your heir, Catullus. Still,
I won't believe it till I read the will.

## 12.76

A jar of wine costs twenty cents; a peck of wheat costs four.
    The farmer, drunk and overstuffed, has nothing anymore.

## 12.78

I didn't write of you, Bithynicus. You say,
    "I don't believe it—swear!" I'd rather pay.

## 12.79

I've given much you asked me for—
and more. Yet *still* you ask for more.
One, Atticilla, who will stick
at no request will suck a dick.

## 12.80

Callistratus praises all, not those he should.
    If no one's bad, can anyone be good?

## 12.81

For the Saturnalia, Umber used to send me
a light coat as a present. He was poor.
He sends light broth now, for he's poor no more.

## 12.84

Reluctant, Polytimus, to spoil your hair,
    I'm glad now that I yielded to your prayer.
So Pelops shone, new shorn, hair laid aside,
    revealing all his ivory to his bride.

## 12.85

You say the mouths of buggers stink.
Fabullus, if that's true, do tell
where you think pussy-lickers smell.

## 12.86

You've thirty boys and thirty slave girls, too.
    Your only cock won't rise. What will you do?

## 12.87

Cotta complained he'd lost his sandals twice
because of a neglectful slave. He's poor:
that slave is his whole staff. Astute and shrewd,
he found a method of preventing more
losses of what he can't afford to lose:
he started dining out without his shoes.

## 12.91

Magulla, you share your husband's bed
and the boy he sleeps with. Why not, too,

the boy who serves his wine? You sigh.
Aha! You fear he'll poison you.

## 12.92

Priscus, you often ask what I'd be like
　　if I got wealth and power suddenly.
Can anyone foretell his future conduct?
　　If you were a lion, what kind would you be?

## 12.93

Labulla has found a way to kiss
her lover while her husband's by.
She keeps on kissing her fool, a dwarf.
At once, before her kisses dry,
the lover grabs him and sends him back
to the smiling lady, bearing his.
What a great fool the husband is!

## 12.95

Istantius Rufus, read Mussetius'
books of buggery, which vie
with those of Sybaris, their sheets
infused with smutty wit. But try
to have a girl with you, or else
your own licentious hands will sound
the wedding song while you become
a husband with no bride around.

## 12.96

You know your husband's faithfulness and habits,
　　and that no woman shares your marriage bed,
why fret, then, as though pages were your rivals,
　　whose charms are brief and very soon have fled?
Those boys, I'll prove, give *you* more than their master:
　　they make you the sole woman for your mate,

and give what you don't want to. "But I *will*,
    so that his fickle love won't stray," you state.
That's not the same: I want a Chian fig,
    not large ones (and in case you haven't known,
*your* kind is large). A wife should know her limits:
    leave *their* part to the boys, and use your own.

## 12·97

Your wife's the kind of girl a husband hardly
would ask for, Bassus, in his rashest prayer—
rich, noble, cultivated, chaste—and yet
you drain your loins in slave boys with long hair,
purchased with your wife's dowry. That's the reason
the cock she bought for many thousands lies
so weak when it returns that coaxing words
or a soft thumb's request won't make it rise.
Feel shame for once! We'll sue if you withhold it.
Bassus, the penis isn't yours; you sold it.

# Notes

## Book One

1.1.   By the time Martial published book 1 of his epigrams (around 86 CE), he was already well known for his three previous collections: *De Spectaculis* (about the shows at the Colosseum), *Xenia* (mottos to accompany gifts of food or wine), and *Apophoreta* (mottos to accompany presents for the Saturnalia) (Shackleton Bailey 1:2–3).

1.9.   *Bellus*, which could mean "handsome, nice, pleasant," was usually used ironically by Martial (Howell, *Commentary* 128).

1.10.   Martial suggests that Maronilla is rich and consumptive.

1.13.   Pliny, in his *Epistles* 3.16, recounts Arria's suicide after her husband Caecina Paetus was involved in a failed revolt against Emperor Claudius in 42 CE. She stabbed herself and handed the sword to him, saying, "Paete, non dolet" (Paetus, it doesn't hurt) (cited in Howell, *Commentary* 136–37). The rest of the quote in Martial's epigram is his own invention (Howell, *Commentary* 137).

1.16.   The addressee of this poem is Avitus, usually assumed to be L. Stertinius Avitus (Howell, *Commentary* 144), who was consul in 92 CE and is mentioned in Martial's preface to book 9 as wanting to place a bust of Martial in his library (Shackleton Bailey 2:233).

1.17.   This epigram is one of several in which Martial implies that he is being advised to practice law as a way to earn more money. His answer, that a field is splendid if it is tended by a farmer, is his self-deprecatory way of implying that he would not know how to do law, when really it didn't appeal to him.

1.19.   Martial frequently alludes to people who have lost their teeth, some of whom buy false teeth to hide the loss. Aelia is presumably old, so this also is one of Martial's many poems making fun of old women for being unattractive.

1.20.   Emperor Claudius reportedly died after eating mushrooms poisoned by his wife Agrippina. Boletus mushrooms were an expensive delicacy, so for the host to eat the entire serving in front of his guests would be rude (Howell, *Commentary* 151).

1.23.   Martial suggests that Cotta is looking for attractive sexual partners, not just dining companions, at the baths.

1.24.   Decianus, the addressee of this epigram, was a friend of Martial's from Spain (Shackleton Bailey 3:351). M. Curius Dentatus and M. Furius Camillus were heroes of the early Roman Republic, the former ending the Samnite Wars and the latter fighting off an invasion of Gauls (Howell, *Commentary* 159–60). Martial is here satirizing a man whose show of stern virtue and disregard for his appearance is meant to conceal the fact that he allows himself to be sodomized (Shackleton Bailey 1:58n), behavior that was considered shameful and unmanly.

1.27.   The Greek proverb quoted means "I hate a fellow-drinker who remembers things" (Howell, *Commentary* 43).

1.28.   Because *acerra* means "incense-casket," the name Acerra suits a person who reeks (Howell, *Commentary* 167).

1.29.   Fidentinus, whose name (from the word *fidens*, meaning "bold") suggests shamelessness (Howell, *Commentary* 168), is advised to pay Martial off if he doesn't wish to be exposed as a plagiarist.

1.30.   The joke here is that since Diaulus killed his patients, he is better qualified to be a mortician. Jokes about deadly doctors are common in Martial.

1.32.   Although it is possible that Martial is just pretending not to know the reason for his dislike (so as not to name a shocking cause), it seems more likely that the poem is concerned with instinctive aversion for which there is no obvious cause.

1.33.   Women were expected to mourn demonstratively for their dead relations. Gellia is exposed as a hypocrite because she weeps only in public.

1.34.   As Howell points out, the name Lesbia is clearly borrowed from Catullus and is usually used in erotic contexts by Martial. Summemmi could refer to a brothel owner, the name of a brothel, or its location. Chione is a name Martial often uses for a prostitute, and he here implies that the lowest order of whores service their customers in tombs (Howell, *Commentary* 179–81).

1.37.  The ridiculous luxury of using a golden chamber pot is emphasized by saving the obscenity *cacas* (you shit) for the end of the epigram.

1.38.  Fidentinus, the plagiarist of 1.29, reappears in this epigram, in which he has garbled Martial's poems so badly in reciting them that Martial denies any part in them.

1.40.  Martial's 1.39 had lavishly praised his friend Decianus. Martial imagines his reader reacting negatively to that praise.

1.46.  Shackleton Bailey changes the gender of the name from Hedyle (a masculine name) in the manuscripts to Hedyli (a feminine name), arguing that catamites were generally boy slaves and wouldn't "claim urgent business elsewhere" (1:73n). But prostitutes could be male or female, so the masculine name can fit the context.

1.47.  The doctor of 1.30 reappears here, and the joke is similar.

1.54.  The Fuscus addressed here may be the rich lawyer of that name whom Martial addresses in 7.28 (Howell, *Commentary* 235).

1.57.  Flaccus, the addressee of this poem, appears to have been a close friend of Martial's and is addressed twenty-one times in his epigrams (Howell, *Commentary* 242).

1.58.  Phoebus may have earned his money by marrying a wealthy wife, though payment for other sexual activity is not ruled out.

1.59.  The dole (*sportula*) was the amount patrons gave to their clients in lieu of a small basket of food; the amount (one hundred quadrantes, or about twenty-five sesterces) would not have gone far in a luxury resort such as Baiae (Shackleton Bailey 1:85n). Located in the volcanic region near Naples, Baiae had hot springs of sulfurous water that was reputed to be curative (Howell, *Commentary* 245). The baths of Lupus and Gryllus were presumably a small, ill-lit private establishment in Rome (247).

1.62.  The fashionable resort of Baiae, known for its luxurious baths, sulfur-laden waters, and nearby lakes, was also famous for the sybaritic and loose behavior of the Romans who visited it (Howell, *Commentary* 245–46). Martial often refers to Sabine women as stern exemplars of morality. In Homer's *Odyssey*, Penelope was the epitome of what a faithful wife should be, whereas Helen started the Trojan war by abandoning her husband Menelaus to run off with handsome young Paris.

1.63.  The name Celer, which means "hasty," may have been chosen to suggest the impatience of the addressee to read his own verse.

1.64.  By praising herself, Fabulla makes her other assets less attractive.

1.71.  The number of drafts swallowed is equal to the number of letters in the name of each girl. Each draft (*cyathus* in Latin) is about a twelfth of a pint (Shackleton Bailey 1:95n), so he has consumed about a quart of Falernian (a high-quality wine) by the end of the poem and is ready to sleep. Romans often drank to the health of their beloved (Howell, *Commentary* 272), but the number of girls mentioned and the fact that none will come to the speaker is meant to be funny. Martial regularly jokes about being turned down by prostitutes.

1.72. Fidentinus is again mentioned as a plagiarist (as in 1.29 and 1.38). He is compared to an old woman who buys false teeth carved of ivory or bone, and to a dark-skinned woman who uses powdered white lead to look fairer. Martial implies that in the future Fidentinus will buy a wig once he becomes bald.

1.73. The implied irony is that the wife of Caecilianus is not very good-looking, but that his jealous protection of her backfires because it is taken as a challenge by the local seducers.

1.74. Martial implies that by marrying the man with whom she formerly committed adultery, Paula confirms the affair that she previously could deny.

1.77. The pallor of Charinus is presented as a mystery, since each of the possible causes (disease, heavy drinking, bad digestion, little sun) is ruled out. It is even implied that he is trying to conceal the pallor by getting a tan and using rouge. But the last line provides the solution to the riddle. Romans believed that performing cunnilingus was not only shameful but caused an unhealthy pallor, so the "and yet" of the last line is ironic (Howell, *Commentary* 280–81).

1.83. Martial suggests that licking Manneia's mouth is as bad as eating shit because she performs oral sex (Howell, *Commentary* 287). Martial regularly implies that oral sex makes the mouth of the one who performs it smelly or unclean.

1.84. *Pater familiae* means "head (literally, father) of the household," but *familia* could also mean the slaves of the household, so the word is a pun (Shackleton Bailey 1:104n). Though the sons of a knight would normally be knights (*equites*) themselves, because they are born of slave mothers, they are *vernae* (home-born slaves) (Howell, *Commentary* 288).

1.89. Most people would speak praise of Caesar loudly in order to sound loyal, but Cinna is so accustomed to whispering that he can't speak up even when it might do him good (Howell, *Commentary* 297).

1.90. Though Bassa seems to be chaste because she avoids men, she is revealed to be a lesbian with an outsized clitoris which enables her to imitate intercourse (Shackleton Bailey 1:109n). Lucretia was a chaste, noble Roman wife who committed suicide to salvage her honor after she was raped by Sextus Tarquinius. The Theban riddle mentioned is the one that the Sphinx asked Oedipus: "What goes on four legs in the morning, two legs at noon, and three legs in the evening?" The answer is "Man, who crawls as a baby, walks upright when mature, and needs a cane when old." Bassa represents an equally baffling paradox.

1.91. Martial tends to be satirical about critics of his verse who don't publish their own, implying that their verse can't be good if they are unwilling to have others see it.

1.94. Howell suggests that Aegle, a name Martial uses elsewhere for a prostitute, had a bad voice when she was young, because of her sexual activity, which Romans thought affected the voice. At the time, her beauty compensated for it. When she was no longer attractive, her voice improved, but she turned to fellatio as a specialty and therefore could not be kissed (Howell, *Commentary* 304–5).

1.95. Though lawyers might bring their clients to court or pay others to applaud their own speeches or to heckle their opponents, Aelius seems to be freelancing by interrupting lawyers in the hope of being paid to shut up (Howell, *Commentary* 305).

1.102. Martial implies that the painter deliberately made Venus look bad to flatter Minerva, who had lost to Venus in the beauty contest judged by Paris. The addressee of this poem is Lycoris. Howell points out that her Greek name suggests that she is a prostitute, whose association with the goddess Venus would be obvious (Howell, *Commentary* 317).

1.105. Howell states that the addressee, Quintus Ovidius, a friend and patron of Martial's, owned a place near Martial's Nomentan farm, and both would have produced wine from their own vineyards. Martial here jokes that if you keep Nomentan wine long enough, you can pass it off as a more illustrious vintage (Howell, *Commentary* 323–25).

1.106. Howell argues that, though it was customary to drink wine mixed with water, Rufus is apparently adding an excessive amount of water to a very small amount of wine. Martial jokes that Rufus must be staying sober to better enjoy a night of sex with Naevia. When Rufus sighs and refuses to answer, Martial concludes that Rufus has been refused (making his self-denial even odder) and urges him to get drunk quickly by drinking unmixed wine, a practice generally frowned on as excessive (Howell, *Commentary* 325–27).

1.108.   Martial's home on the Quirinal hill overlooked the Campus of Vipsanius Agrippa to the west (Shackleton Bailey 1:123n). This poem is an apology for ducking the expected (and onerous) morning calls of a client at a patron's house, though Martial expresses a willingness to show up for a meal later in the day. Meanwhile, he offers his book as a substitute for showing up in person in the mornings.

1.110.   Velox, which means "speedy," is a suitable name for a man who can't stand long epigrams.

1.111.   M. Aquilius Regulus was a lawyer and a patron of Martial's (Shackleton Bailey 3:379). This poem would have accompanied a gift of this book and incense to his patron (1:127n).

1.112.   Martial hoped that Priscus would become his patron, but has been disappointed (Shackleton Bailey 1:127n).

1.113.   Under the cover of self-deprecating comments about his earlier poems and juvenilia, Martial advertises where they can be bought.

1.117.   Shackleton Bailey notes that Ad Pirum (At the Pear Tree) is the name of the apartment building in which Martial lives; Argiletum is a street of shops near the Forum Julium; and five denarii is the equivalent of twenty sesterces (1:131n). The edges of a papyrus scroll would be smoothed by being rubbed with pumice, and the parchment case of a deluxe copy would be stained purple (Howell, *Commentary* 351). Martial repeatedly makes fun of people too cheap to buy his book, who prefer to borrow a copy or ask Martial to give them one for free (as in 4.72).

# Book Two

2.3.   Martial observes that Sextus cannot be considered a debtor if he will never be able to pay off his loan.

2.4.   The terms "sister" and "brother" were often used as terms of affection and could be used toward a girlfriend or boyfriend (Williams 35). Both the intimacy of the terms and their blurring of the generational gap suggest an over-eroticized and possibly incestuous relationship between mother and son.

2.5.   Decianus was a friend of Martial's from Emerita in Spain (Shackleton Bailey 3:351), and is also addressed in 1.24. Though Decianus appears to be a patron as well, the implied criticism of him for turning a friend away is offset by Martial's stated eagerness to see his friend and willingness to go long distances to do so (Williams 37).

2.10.  Romans often greeted friends or acquaintances with a kiss. Martial turns the tables on someone who kisses him in a perfunctory or condescending way by implying that the kisses aren't wanted anyway. As is usual in Martial, to suggest that someone's mouth is repellent implies that the person performs oral sex (Williams 55).

2.12.  In this epigram, Martial implies that Postumus tries to use perfume to disguise the smelly mouth he gets from performing oral sex.

2.13.  Martial jokes that it would be cheaper to pay off a debt than to go to court about the matter and have to pay a rapacious lawyer and bribe the judge.

2.15.  It was customary to pass cups for a toast. The fact that Hormus won't share his could be considered arrogant, but Martial suggests that Hormus is doing people a favor because his mouth is disgusting, presumably from performing oral sex (Williams 76).

2.17.  Subura was an area of Rome known for prostitution; according to Shackleton Bailey, the fact that the woman is sitting suggests that she is a prostitute. The verb *tondere* means both "to clip" and "to rob," and *radere* means "to shave" but can also have the meaning of "to fleece someone" (1:147n).

2.19.  Martial is insulting the meager dinners that Zoilus provides to his guests. Williams notes that Aricia, sixteen miles outside of Rome on the Appian Way, was a place that beggars congregated. Roman diners reclined on couches while eating, but the beggars, of course, would be lying on the ground (90–91).

2.20.  Martial is playing on the idea that once you buy something, you can call it yours. As Williams notes, there was no copyright on creative works, so plagiarism would have been easy (91). Martial defends his work by satirizing the plagiarists.

2.21.  The addressee of this poem is Postumus (presumably the same one mentioned in 2.10 and 2.12). The implied point again is that Martial would prefer to avoid the kisses of a man who performs oral sex.

2.22.  The apostrophe to Phoebus and the Muses uses inflated language for humorous effect. This poem alludes to 2.10 and implies that Martial's fame from his poetry is what is bringing him unwanted attentions from Postumus.

2.23. Martial plays along with readers' assumptions that the name Postumus is a pseudonym for a real person, but refuses to reveal his identity for fear of being kissed even more often in revenge.

2.25. Martial frequently uses logic to twist someone's refusal of his request into an acceptance (Williams 102).

2.26. Bithynicus is wooing Naevia, who pretends to be consumptive in order to lead him on. She presumably has money, and he wants to marry her in the hope that she will die soon. Another possible explanation advanced by Williams is that he is being attentive to her in the hope of getting a legacy from her (104).

2.27. Selius earns his dinner by loudly praising the performance of his patron in court or at a poetry reading. It was common practice for advocates to bring their clients into the courtroom to provide vocal support for the patrons' arguments, in the hope of swaying the decision.

2.28. Williams notes that the other two options that Martial hasn't mentioned are that Sextillus performs fellatio or cunnilingus. What starts out looking like a defense of Sextillus turns into a riddle whose solution is even more shameful than the initial accusation. Giving someone the middle finger, then as now, was an aggressive sexual gesture, which turns the accusation back on the accuser (109–10).

2.30. Gaius, a rich friend of longstanding who increases his wealth by lending money, is asked to lend Martial an amount of money that Martial protests is small for someone like Gaius. Instead of lending the money, he tells Martial to earn more by becoming a lawyer (as Titus had advised Martial in 1.17). As in the earlier epigram, Martial has no interest in a career as an advocate.

2.31. Literally, Martial is saying "nothing can surpass it," which wouldn't be very funny if it just means that she is very good, so I am taking it to mean that she does all that is humanly possible.

2.33. Philaenis is apparently an old woman who is bald, red-faced, and one-eyed. At first Martial just seems to be making fun of her for being ugly, but the joke turns out to be that those characteristics are shared by a penis, and that kissing her would be the equivalent of performing fellatio (Williams 128–29).

2.38. Martial often refers to his farm in Nomentum, some twenty kilometers northeast of Rome (Williams 142). Though in other poems he complains that its yield is modest, in this one he puts down the nosy Linus by retorting that the farm at least provides an escape from *him*.

2.39. Roman law required prostitutes and convicted adulteresses to wear togas (Shackleton Bailey 1:161n). The adulteress in this poem is notorious, but not convicted.

2.42. Martial implies that the head of Zoilus is dirtier than his ass because he performs oral sex (Williams 155).

2.49. Telesina is an adulteress, so Martial at first rejects her as a potential wife. However, she has sex with boys. Williams points out that Roman tradition allowed a man who discovered his wife having sex with a boy to bugger the boy as punishment, so a wife who sleeps with boys would bring many opportunities for sex with boys. Martial is poking fun at himself by implying that he would be willing to tolerate adultery for that reason (176).

2.50. Martial implies that Lesbia's habit of drinking water (instead of wine) is appropriate, since she performs fellatio and therefore needs to wash her mouth out. As usual, Martial presents oral sex as being unclean (Williams 177).

2.51. Hyllus is down to his last denarius, but would rather spend it on being sodomized than on eating. It was considered shameful for a man to be sodomized, and Hyllus is also being satirized for being poor, being sexually voracious, and having to pay to be sodomized (Williams 179).

2.52. Williams notes that Dasius, the owner or manager of the baths, charges three times the usual entrance fee to Spatale, making her pay separately for each of her breasts. The joke is aimed both at the enterprisingly venal Dasius and at Spatale, who by paying acknowledges that the charge is appropriate (181–83).

2.53. Though one might assume at first that Maximus is a slave, his drinking wine and using prostitutes shows that he is not; instead, he feels burdened by his duties as a client, which also provide him with luxuries he cannot otherwise afford. Williams notes that Martial repeatedly uses the wine of Veii as an example of bad wine drunk by the poor (185) and that two asses (bronze coins of low value) was a low price for an ordinary prostitute (185). Kings of Parthia, an enemy country in the region that now includes Iran (186), would be associated with wealth and luxury, like other eastern monarchs.

2.54. The epigram suggests that the wife of Linus knows that he likes to be sodomized and that that is why she sets a eunuch (who could not do it) to watch him. Martial pretends to sympathize with Linus for having such a nosy and malicious wife, who treats her husband as if he were a wife by setting a eunuch to guard him (Williams 187).

2.55. Williams observes that Sextus wants flattery and attention from Martial as a client, rather than the affection of a friend, which Martial wants to give him. By emphasizing his superior status, Sextus can demand the flattery, but he loses the friendship (189).

2.56. This poem gives an interesting twist to the usual charge of corruption among provincial Roman officials. Williams observes that Gallus, a Roman official in Libya, has brought his wife along, though it was more customary to leave wives behind when stationed abroad. She is charged with greed, which would normally imply accepting bribes. Martial denies that she takes anything, but insists instead that she gives—implying sexual favors (191). Since the word *gallus* could mean a eunuch priest of Cybele (Williams 166), the husband's name in this epigram may also suggest that his wife is turning to foreign lovers because her husband cannot satisfy her.

2.58. Martial suggests that Zoilus bought his toga with borrowed money that has not been repaid (Sullivan 244). A new toga would have a fleecy nap, which would be worn off in an old one (Williams 197).

2.59. Shackleton Bailey notes that Domitian had built a little banqueting hall called Mica Aureus ("The Golden Crumb") overlooking the Mausoleum of Augustus, in which the Caesars had been buried. Augustus was deified after his death, hence the irony that even a god can die (1:175n). Nard was a perfume made from spikenard and often applied to the hair at banquets, when rose garlands would also be worn (Williams 200). The poem exhorts readers to make the most of physical pleasures because life is short.

2.60. Williams notes that this poem refers to a recent law of Domitian's prohibiting castration. Hyllus, who is committing adultery with a tribune's wife, expects, if he is caught, to receive the punishment reserved for boys breaking a law: to be sodomized (201–2). When he protests that castration is against the law, Martial points out that Hyllus too is breaking a law and therefore shouldn't expect legal protection.

2.61. Williams notes that the unnamed target of this poem performed fellatio while still young; now that he is so repulsive that he is scorned even by paupers' undertakers and public executioners (professions that were considered unclean), he spitefully uses his tongue to slander everyone. Martial raises the usual assumption that performing oral sex is a filthy act, then turns it around by saying that slandering others is even filthier; unlike the epigram's target, Martial does not name names in his attacks, or the names he gives are pseudonyms (203–5).

2.62. Williams points out that Labienus is going to extremes by depilating his chest, arms, legs and genitals, though his professed reason is to please his mistress. That he also depilates his buttocks, however, suggests that he likes to be buggered, which was considered a shameful taste in a man. Though his claims about the mistress may be intentional misdirection, many men of the time were bisexual. It was only being penetrated during sex that was considered effeminate (207–8).

2.63. Milichus, though he has only one hundred thousand sesterces left, has spent them all to buy a female slave as a sex partner. Williams states that such a sum was extremely high, but not unheard of for a desirable slave. Martial assumes that love would be the only explanation for such extravagance, but Milichus denies that he loves her, which makes his behavior even more spendthrift (209).

2.65. This poem contains a twofold joke. First, Martial implies that Saleianus' show of mourning for the death of his rich wife is hypocritical, which Martial subtly satirizes with his melodramatic exclamations about the death. Then, Martial's last line appears to be condoling with the grieving husband while actually expressing regret at his good fortune.

2.66. Lalage loses her temper when one ringlet of an elaborate hairdo is out of place, so she beats the offending slave girl who has done her hair, using the polished bronze mirror in which she has seen the offending curl. Martial suggests that Lalage deserves to be burned with a curling iron (called a salamander because, like the mythical creature of that name, it could withstand the fire) or have her head shaved so that her appearance would be as ugly as her behavior.

2.67. Because Postumus mindlessly repeats the standard greeting ("How are you doing?"), no matter how often in an hour he meets Martial, Martial concludes that Postumus has nothing to do himself.

2.68. Williams notes that, as a former client of Olus, Martial used to address him as "lord" and "patron," but now declares his independence by calling Olus by name. The *pilleum* was a felt cap worn by freed slaves. Martial will give up the dole from his patron, even if it means living in poverty (220–21).

2.70. Martial satirizes Cotilus for his presumed fastidiousness about bathing in water that has washed penises (an image sexualized by saying that the water has been forced to suck penises), pointing out that Cotilus himself can't bathe without washing his penis before his head (Williams 225).

2.71. Martial pretends to believe that Caecilianus is reading epigrams by Catullus and Marsus (famous masters of the form) to make Martial's epigrams look better by comparison, though clearly Caecilianus is actually trying to make Martial's poems look bad. By suggesting that Caecilianus read his own poems instead, Martial implies that they are so bad that they would *really* make Martial's look better.

2.73. This epigram appears as a single line in the manuscript, but a preceding line is often supplied by editors to fill out the implied meaning of the poem (Williams 231). Lyris claims that she cannot tell what she is doing when she is drunk, but Martial implies that she might be lying to save face. He informs her that she performs fellatio when drunk—just as she does when sober.

2.76. Legacy-seekers were often disappointed when they gave gifts to wealthy people in the hope of a postmortem bonanza. Here Martial mockingly claims to be shocked at the perfidy of Marius for leaving a legacy to someone who never gave him anything (Shackleton Bailey 1:188n).

2.78. The addressee of this poem, Caecilianus, is being accused of stinginess for not heating his warm bath properly for his guests (Shackleton Bailey 1:189n).

2.79. Martial implies that Nasica has been deliberately inviting Martial to dinner on occasions that he knows Martial is entertaining and can't come. In retaliation, Martial declines a dinner invitation from Nasica by saying he has a pressing engagement—to dine at home (Shackleton Bailey 1:190n).

2.80. The word *hostem* (foes) suggests an enemy army, so Fannius is presumably running from battle, not from the law (Shackleton Bailey 1:191n).

2.83. Williams notes that cutting off the nose and ears of an adulterer caught in the act was a well-known punishment, but, as Martial points out, it does not prevent the adulterer from continuing to have sex with the wife. The epigram adds an unexpected, lurid twist by suggesting that the sex might include fellatio, a further shame to the husband (253–54).

2.87. Sextus claims to have young beauties on fire with love for him, yet he has the puffy face of a man holding his breath underwater. Martial implies that Sextus is lying.

2.88. Mamercus, a would-be poet, recites none of his poems, the usual way to establish a reputation as a poet (Williams 266). Martial satirically suggests that Mamercus can keep claiming to be a poet, so long as he recites nothing. Either the poems would definitively prove that he is no poet, or they are so bad that Martial would rather hear the boasts than the poems.

2.89. Williams notes that the practice of citing precedents was common in rhetoric, and here Martial borrows it under the pretense of excusing a series of bad habits of Gaurus. But when he comes to fellatio, he cannot recall any famous possessors of that habit (267).

2.92. Martial likes to boast that the emperor has accorded him the same rights that a father of three children had. Here he claims that he will say farewell to his wife, since to have a wife might make the emperor's gift unnecessary. As Williams notes, most scholars doubt that Martial was ever married, so the "wife" he addresses is likely just a potential wife. In some poems Martial adopts the persona of a married man for comic purposes (279–80).

2.93. M. Aquilius Regulus, an advocate and patron of Martial's (Shackleton Bailey 3:379), had apparently not been given book 1, possibly because Martial has no copies left to give him (1:199n). Williams suggests that the "modesty" of book 1 was either that it was not worthy to be presented or that it didn't call itself "Book I," which would imply that others would follow (281–82). Martial jokingly proposes that the title can be changed by dropping one I from the Roman numeral II.

# Book Three

3.3. The poem appears to be set at a spa, and the goddess mentioned is probably the nymph of the spring. Though people typically bathed naked, the unnamed addressee is advised to wear her tunic to hide her ugly body. The salve on her face was probably intended, like a modern mudpack, to improve the complexion.

3.6. It was customary for young men to dedicate the first shaving of their beards to a god, to mark their entrance into manhood (Shackleton Bailey 1:205n). Marcellinus was a soldier and a friend of Martial's (3:366).

3.8. The name Thais is associated with prostitutes, including, famously, a courtesan of Alexander the Great. Having one eye is among the physical disabilities that Martial mocks most often.

3.9. Although there was a famous poet named Cinna, a friend of Catullus, the Cinna in this poem has published nothing and, according to Martial, never will.

3.12. Catullus, in his poem 13, invites his friend Fabullus to dinner but warns him to bring the food and wine himself, offering to provide in return some of the perfume of his beloved Lesbia. Martial in this poem jokes that offering perfume and no dinner is suitable for a corpse, which would be anointed to cover the smell of decomposition.

3.14.   The dole (*sportula*) was originally a basket of food given by patrons to their clients; later, small amounts of money (about twenty-five sesterces) would be given instead (Shackleton Bailey 1:85n). The dole was apparently abolished by law around the time this book was written, but seems to have been reinstated later (1:206n). The Mulvian Bridge was outside the Porta Flaminia, on the north side of Rome (1:211n).

3.15.   This poem puns on two meanings of "credit": personal trust and financial lending (Shackleton Bailey 1:211n).

3.17.   Martial suggests that the mouth of Sabidius is unclean from performing oral sex, and that his blowing on the tart therefore pollutes it so that no one else will eat it.

3.18.   Recitation of poems at dinners was a form of entertainment and a way that Romans made a name for themselves as poets. Readers may suspect that the excuse of Maximus is false modesty and that Martial calls his bluff or that Martial expects a poor reading and therefore is looking for a way to avoid it.

3.22.   M. Gavius Apicius, who lived in the time of Augustus and Tiberius, was famous for his extravagance in pursuit of fine dining (Shackleton Bailey 3:340).

3.26.   Murrine was an expensive stone, possibly fluorspar, used to make ornamental carved cups and vessels (Shackleton Bailey 1:221n).

3.27.   Martial suggests that Gallus is snubbing him by not inviting him back after repeated dinner invitations from Martial. Martial turns the joke on himself as well, implying he's a fool to let Gallus take advantage of him.

3.28.   Martial suggests that Nestor has either bad breath or an unclean mouth from performing oral sex.

3.32.   Hecuba was turned into a bitch by rage after losing her children. Niobe was turned to stone from grief after losing hers. Martial often jokes about the temptation to make money by marrying a rich old woman, but he always presents the option as unappealing; there is no evidence that he ever married.

3.33.   There is more prestige to having freeborn sexual partners, but Martial implies that looks trump status every time.

3.34.   Chione, a Greek name, suggests that the addressee is likely to be a prostitute. Fair skin was considered more desirable than dark skin, a fact that Martial alludes to often.

3.37. This poem implies that wealthy patrons use pretended offenses as excuses not to be generous with their gifts. As a satirist, Martial may have had patrons who thought his attacks were aimed at them, though he insisted that he never targeted individuals.

3.39. Lycoris, a Greek name, often is used by Martial for a prostitute; Ganymede was a Trojan prince so handsome that he was abducted by Jove to be his cupbearer and catamite. Martial's humor frequently targets physical disabilities. Faustinus was a wealthy friend whom Martial addresses or refers to nineteen times in his poems (Howell, *Commentary* 161).

3.41. Martial often jokes about being unable to repay the loans he gets from patrons. Here, because he does pay the loan back, he jokes that *he* is the one doing his patron a favor.

3.43. Proserpina is the Roman goddess of the dead, who is not fooled about the true age of Laetinus. The mask described is the kind used by actors, worn with a wig to cover the entire head.

3.45. Thyestes was tricked into eating his own sons by his brother Atreus, who chopped them up, cooked them, and served them to their father. Phoebus Apollo, the sun god, was so appalled at the sight that he reversed his course (Shackleton Bailey 3:342). Ligurinus tries to attract willing listeners by inviting them to a lavish dinner of delicacies: expensive fish, oysters, and mushrooms. But the good food cannot compensate for his dreadful poetry.

3.48. Shackleton Bailey notes that a "pauper's cell" was a small, meagerly furnished room in a rich man's house, a novel contrast to the usual luxury of the place. Though Olus has not literally become a pauper, he has foolishly transformed his valuable land into something worthless (1:235n).

3.49. Martial often mentions Veientan wine as a bad wine and Massic as an excellent one. The host is being satirized for serving his guests wine much worse than he himself is drinking.

3.51. Martial implies that Galla must have some physical flaws she is trying to hide by not bathing with him (Shackleton Bailey 1:237n).

3.53. Chloe's Greek name suggests that she is a prostitute.

3.54. Galla is an expensive prostitute. Martial asks her to refuse him so that he will not have to admit that he cannot afford her.

3.55. Cosmus is mentioned in many of Martial's epigrams as a perfumer (Shackleton Bailey 3:350). Martial implies that Gellia may use perfume not just to be fashionable, but to cover up offensive body odor.

3.57. Ravenna was suffering from such a drought that Martial jokes that innkeepers would cheat their customers not by overwatering the wine, as usual, but by serving the wine neat. Romans did not usually drink wine that had not been diluted with water.

3.61. Martial puns on two meanings of "denying nothing": "giving everything" and "denying even the request for nothing." Cinna is labeled *improbus* (i.e., dishonest) for pretending that his requests are minimal when they are not.

3.64. This poem, addressed to Martial's friend Cassianus, is a compliment to another friend, Canius Rufus of Gades (in Spain), an author mentioned in several of Martial's epigrams (Shackleton Bailey 3:346). The sirens, part bird, part woman, were deadly dangers that Ulysses (Odysseus) managed to escape by putting wax in his men's ears and having them tie him to the mast of his ship as he sailed past. Martial is implying that Canius is even more riveting as a storyteller than the Sirens were as singers.

3.65. Diadumenus, the addressee here and in 5.46 and 6.34, appears to be a boy slave of Martial's (Shackleton Bailey 3:352).

3.68. Martial here signals a switch to more obscene epigrams in the latter half of the book, poking fun at Roman matrons whose pose of modesty, he suggests, covers a fascination with the obscene material in which they are supposed to have no interest. According to Shackleton Bailey, there is no record elsewhere of the ceremony of Venus mentioned in the poem (1:252n). The object that Venus welcomes in the rite is clearly a representation of a penis; statues of Priapus, who is portrayed with an oversized penis, were placed in gardens to protect them from thieves. Terpsichore, the Muse of dancing, here symbolizes the dancing girls and prostitutes that would have entertained men at drinking parties.

3.69. While purporting to praise the innocuous poems of Cosconius, Martial makes his own sound much more appealing. Martial often feels the need to defend his poems from attacks on their obscenity. Here his argument is that he is suiting his language to his intended audience.

3.70. The addressee of this poem is Scaevinus, whose name comes from *scaevus*, a Latin word meaning "perverse."

3.71. Naevolus is accused of enjoying being buggered, which was considered shameful.

3.72. Martial implies that Saufeia's false modesty either is a cover for deformity or is foolish because it leads him to that assumption as the only possible explanation for her contradictory behavior.

3.73. This poem poses a riddle: if Phoebus is sleeping with well-hung boys, but is impotent himself, one might assume that he enjoys being buggered, but rumor denies that. What other alternative is there? Only the even more disreputable one that he enjoys performing fellatio.

3.76. Andromache was Hector's beautiful wife in *The Iliad* and Hecuba was his ancient mother.

3.79. Martial often takes an odd behavioral quirk, as here, and extends it to the point of absurdity.

3.80. Apicius has a wicked tongue, Martial implies, because he performs oral sex.

3.83. Chione is a Greek name that Martial often uses for prostitutes. In 3.87 he uses that name for a prostitute who performs fellatio. For a poet to be told to imitate a prostitute is insulting, but Martial replies that he can't possibly match her for speed.

3.84. Martial is punning on the fact that *linguam* (tongue) is a feminine noun when he implies not that Gongylion's wife has a female lover, but that Gongylion's own tongue is her lover.

3.86. In poem 3.68 Martial had warned chaste matrons to read no further in book 3 because what followed would be openly obscene poems. Here he pretends to have caught the ladies still reading, but he argues that the mimes that ladies would see in the theater are just as obscene as anything in his book.

3.87. Martial presents a paradox: Chione has never been fucked and wears a loincloth at the public baths in a show of excessive modesty, yet she is shameless. He implies that she performs fellatio, and therefore shouldn't show her face in public.

3.88. This poem is an example of Martial's love of seeming contradictions.

3.89. Soft mallows and lettuce, Martial suggests, were used as cures for constipation, but Martial is probably making fun of the facial expression of Phoebus, not offering helpful dietary hints.

3.90. Shackleton Bailey points out that *quid sibi velit* can mean both "what she means" and "what she wants for herself" (1:267n).

3.94. Martial may be implying that the host is cheap, as well as irascible, and that he is using the undercooked hare as an excuse not to serve anything. The Latin name Rufus (which means "red") would suit an angry man.

3.96. Shackleton Bailey suggests that Gargilius would not be talking because he would be forced to perform fellatio on the speaker as a punishment (1:273n). Another possible explanation is that the speaker would cut out the tongue of Gargilius.

3.100. Martial here seems to be indulging in self-deprecatory modesty in saying that his book deserves to be washed out, though that may be because of the obscenity that he has acknowledged in it.

# Book Four

4.6. Stella, a patron of Martial's, wrote elegiac poetry himself, so to recite the same kind of poetry while a guest in his house would be insulting to him (Shackleton Bailey 1:282n).

4.7. Hyllus is here presumed to be a boy slave of Martial's, and is trying to get out of having to have sex with him by claiming to have reached manhood. Though sex with boys was customary and accepted, sex with grown men was frowned on (Moreno Soldevila 133).

4.12. Thais is a name often used by Martial for prostitutes. The fact that she doesn't draw the line at fellatio puts her among the most debased prostitutes.

4.13. The addressee of this poem, Rufus, has not been identified, since there are several men named Rufus in Martial's poems, some real and some apparently invented (Moreno Soldevila 167). Aulus Pudens was a friend of Martial's (Shackleton Bailey 3:378). Hymen is the god of marriage, and torches were part of the wedding procession, accompanying the bride from her home to her husband's (Moreno Soldevila 169). Nard and cinnamon were both used in perfumes, and honey was often mixed into wine. Martial refers to Massic wine as being one of the best wines, and the honey from the region around Athens, home of Theseus, was also renowned. Grape vines were often trained to grow up elms, so the elm and vine together were a symbol of marriage in Roman times (171–72).

4.15. The platter and serving tools would have been made of silver and therefore worth more than the amount of the original loan request (Moreno Soldevila 188).

4.16. M. Tullius Cicero was the famous orator and statesman of Republican times. M. Aquilius Regulus was a famed contemporary advocate and a patron of Martial's (Shackleton Bailey 3:379). Romans defined incest as including relatives by marriage, not just by blood, so Martial is implying that the relationship between stepmother and stepson is incestuous and was probably adulterous when the father of Gallus was alive (Moreno Soldevila 190).

4.17. Moreno Soldevila notes that the Greek name Lycisca suggests that its owner is a prostitute. Paulus is inciting Martial to write poems attacking her character in order to shame her and make her angry. Martial suggests, however, that Paulus wants to shame her not because he disapproves of her performing fellatio, but because he wants to make her lose other customers (including, possibly, Martial himself) so that Paulus can have her to himself (Moreno Soldevila 195–96).

4.20. Shackleton Bailey identifies the addressee, Collinus, as a poet who had won the Capitoline poetry contest (3:349), which was founded by Domitian and held every five years (1:276–77n). The contrast between a young woman who wants to pretend she's older and the old woman who wants to pretend she's younger is typical of Martial's irony. *Pupa* literally means "doll," but is used metaphorically for an attractive woman (Moreno Soldevila 212).

4.21. Martial purports to take it as ironic confirmation of the atheistic views of Segius that such a wicked man is prospering.

4.22. For the purposes of this erotic epigram, Martial pretends to be a newly married husband.

4.24. There is no evidence that Martial ever married, but he sometimes speaks as if he were married, in order to exploit satirical humor about wives and marriage. Fabianus is the addressee of this poem; Shackleton Bailey assumes he is an invented figure, not an actual friend of Martial's (3:354).

4.26. Martial implies that Postumus is so stingy a patron that it is not worth the trouble to be his client. One would have to wear a toga to pay morning calls, so the rewards from Postumus in a year do not even cover the cost of the necessary wardrobe.

4.27. One of the gifts Domitian (here referred to by his title Augustus) gave Martial was the Right of Three Children (Shackleton Bailey 1:299n). This poem is both a thanks to the Emperor and a graceful way to beg for more gifts.

4.29. Aulus Pudens was a friend of Martial, who mentions him in sixteen epigrams (Howell, *Commentary* 172). As the number of his books increased, Martial seems to have worried that their frequency would lower their esteem and make them be taken for granted. I follow Shackleton Bailey's hypothesis that Martial is ranking the satirist Persius, who wrote a book of satires under Nero (3:375), and Marsus the epigrammatist (3:366) as if their books were scoring points in a game (1:300n).

4.32. Amber is called Phaethon's drop because of the myth that after Phaethon was killed by a thunderbolt from Jupiter his grieving sisters were turned into poplar trees, whose weeping sap became amber (recounted in book two of Ovid's *Metamorphoses*).

4.33. What looks like a compliment to Sosibianus for his poetry is actually a sly way of wishing he were dead (Shackleton Bailey 1:305n).

4.34. This riddling epigram implies that the toga is cold because it is threadbare (Shackleton Bailey 1:305n). Martial plays on the fact that snow may not be white, but is always cold.

4.36. Shackleton Bailey hypothesizes that Olus can't dye his beard because of a skin disease (1:305n).

4.38. Galla is a name often used by Martial for prostitutes. Martial suggests that playing hard to get can make a woman more attractive, but can be carried too far.

4.41. Presumably, the person about to recite has a cold and is trying to protect his throat by wrapping it in a scarf. But hoarseness is not desirable in a speaker (Moreno Soldevila 307). The poem also hints that the work to be recited is not worth hearing.

4.43. According to Shackleton Bailey, Pontia and Metilius were well-known poisoners (1:311n). Cybele, the Mother Goddess, was identified with the Syrian goddess Atargetis (1:312n) and was associated with Berecynthus, a region in Phrygia where she was worshiped (3:343). Cybele was thought to afflict wrongdoers with tumors (1:312n), and her priests castrated themselves in a fit of madness sent by the goddess (Moreno Soldevila 323). In swearing by these tumors and frenzies, Martial is wishing them on himself if he is lying (319).

4.44. Vesuvius erupted in 79 CE, destroying Pompeii, whose patron goddess was Venus, and Herculaneum, which was dedicated to Hercules. There was also a famous temple to Venus in Sparta (Shackleton Bailey 1:313n). Nysa was the mountain where the god Bacchus was raised (Moreno Soldevila 329). Martial implies that the gods wish it had not been in their power to destroy places so dear to them. Since Martial reports visits of his to Baiae, a resort on the bay of Naples, he would have seen the volcano Vesuvius firsthand.

4.47. Moreno Soldevila notes that encaustic painting was done using heated, pigmented wax on a tablet (350–51). Martial is joking that Phaethon, who burned up in lightning sent by Jupiter, didn't deserve to be fired a second time. Shackleton Bailey suggests that there may be a pun as well on the name of a twice-baked bread (1:317n).

4.49. Martial is annoyed that turgid retellings of myth were ranked higher in the literary canon than the satiric epigrams that he wrote, but he counters that his own poems are far more popular with readers. He focuses particularly on writers retelling sensational stories of fathers tricked into eating their own sons (Tereus and Thyestes) or filling in trivial background in stories whose real action happens later (Daedalus and Polyphemus). Martial alludes to the robes with trains that tragic actors wore and the ranting, exaggerated style of acting in tragedies, implicitly contrasting them with the more realistic style of his own work.

4.50. Richlin points out that Martial here is alluding to the assumption that old men were the most likely to need oral sex in order to achieve an erection. Thais, a prostitute, insults Martial by calling him old, so he insults her by pointing out that she performs fellatio (Richlin, "Meaning of *Irrumare*" 44).

4.51. Martial, while pretending to wish Caecilianus well, is actually hoping that he will lose his fortune.

4.56. Gargilianus is angling for large legacies from the people to whom he gives. Martial invites him to learn the true meaning of generosity by giving a gift to Martial, from whom he will get nothing in return.

4.58. Galla has presumably shut herself in a dark room to weep, but Martial suggests that she seeks privacy so that no one will see that she is *not* weeping.

4.59. Since Cleopatra was killed by a viper, it is ironic that a viper should have a tomb more magnificent than hers. The snake described here would have been quite small (Shackleton Bailey 1:327n).

4.63. Nero had tried to have his mother Agrippina drowned by a collapsing boat in the same vicinity (Shackleton Bailey 1:331n).

4.65. This poem is a riddle: How can Philaenis weep from just one eye? The answer is that she has only one.

4.69. The good wines that Martial mentions are Setine and Massic. Papylus is rumored to have poisoned his four wives with wine. Though Martial says he doesn't believe the gossip, by saying he isn't thirsty, he shows that he does.

4.70. The addressee of this poem is Marullinus, presumably a friend of Martial's, though not mentioned in other epigrams. Ammianus, who had been wishing for his father's death, regrets it because he is disinherited. The rope he is left suggests that he is being urged to hang himself for some dreadful offense; epigram 2.4, also about an Ammianus, had implied that he was guilty of incest with his mother (Moreno Soldevila 471).

4.71. Safronius Rufus, a friend of Martial's, is described in 11.103 as being extremely modest, so he would be an ideal addressee for Martial's complaint about the shamelessness of women. For no girl to say no sounds like a positive result for men seeking to sleep with them, but Martial points out that many also don't say yes, but coyly keep the men in suspense (Moreno Soldevila 473).

4.72. Quintus is interested only in free copies of Martial's books. When Martial tells him where he can buy the books, Quintus shows how little interest in the books he actually has. This poem is both an advertisement for Martial's bookseller and a warning to those who might ask Martial for free copies. Copies, which would be expensive to have made, might be given for free to friends and patrons, but Martial's response implies that Quintus is neither (Moreno Soldevila 475–76).

4.75. Moreno Soldevila notes that Mummia Nigrina is being praised for sharing her wealth with her husband Rusticus Antistius. Roman women had the right to inherit their father's wealth, retain part of their dowry in the case of divorce, and make their own financial decisions. That Nigrina makes all of her wealth over to her husband is a sign of her extraordinary love for him, which Martial compares favorably to that of Evadne, who burned herself on the pyre of her husband Capaneus, and of Alcestis, who offered her own life to preserve the life of her husband Admetus when he was due to die (487–90).

4.76. When disappointed by an unnamed stingy lender, Martial suggests that the way to get the amount he wants in the future is to double the amount he asks for.

4.77. Martial jokes that he wants wealth not for his own sake, but to provoke suicide in an envious man.

4.79. Matho is not one of Martial's known friends, and Martial's property outside of Rome is elsewhere said to be in Nomentum (see 2.38), so the incident described in this poem may be invented (Moreno Soldevila 503). The joke is partly that, as a guest, Matho would have had all the benefits of the property without the cost of buying it.

4.81. The epigram mentioned is 4.71. Martial frequently comments in one epigram on the purported reactions of a reader to a previous epigram of his, as in 3.68 and 3.86 (Moreno Soldevila 509).

4.83. Martial loves a paradox, here the irony that Naevolus is only considerate when he is worried.

4.84. The answer to the riddle of how a woman who doesn't fuck can be immodest is that she does something even worse: she performs fellatio.

4.85. Ponticus drinks from a cup made of murrine, a semiprecious stone whose opacity would have hidden that he is drinking higher-quality wine than he is serving his guests. The name Ponticus (meaning "from Pontus," a rich province in Asia Minor) would suit a man who flaunts his wealth.

4.87. Moreno Soldevila notes that calling Bassa "your Bassa" suggests that she is the mistress of Fabullus (534). Bassa pretends to dote on infants and often keeps one near her, not because she likes babies, but so that when she farts she can blame the smell on the child.

# Book Five

5.2. Howell notes that Martial presents this book as one that will contain only clean poems, as a tribute to Domitian in his role of censor, enforcer of public morality. Emperor Domitian added Germanicus to his name after his victory over the Chatti in Germany in 83 CE. Minerva is called "the Cecropian girl" after Cecrops, the first king of Athens (Howell, *Martial: Epigrams V* 79). Domitian considered Minerva, the virgin goddess of wisdom, to be his patron goddess (Shackleton Bailey 1:354n).

5.4. Myrtale's use of laurel to cover the odor of alcohol can't disguise her other symptoms of inebriation. She drinks her wine unmixed with water, which would be typical only of heavy drinkers. Howell notes that the name Myrtale comes from the word for myrtle, a flower associated with Venus. She is therefore likely to be a prostitute (Howell, *Martial: Epigrams V* 80).

5.9. Martial frequently jokes that doctors make their patients worse. Symmachus is a Greek name, as most doctors were Greek (Howell, *Martial: Epigrams V* 85). The number of students he brings with him is probably exaggerated for comic effect.

5.17. Gellia brags of her illustrious ancestors and snubs Martial as a mere knight, saying that she wouldn't marry less than a senator, but actually settles for a *cistiber*, a minor police officer (Shackleton Bailey 1:369n).

5.20. Howell notes that the addressee of this poem, Julius Martialis, was one of Martial's closest and oldest friends, to whom he refers in almost all of his books of epigrams (Howell, *Martial: Epigrams V* 99). The "proud busts" would be the wax images of ancestors that decorated the atrium of a great man's house (100). The campus mentioned is the Campus Martius, where men went to exercise or swim in the Tiber (100). The colonnade would be one of several porticoes built to provide shade on sunny days or shelter from the rain (86). The Virgo is the Aqua Virgo, an aqueduct that brought water to the baths in the Campus Martius (101).

5.32.   Faustinus, the addressee of this poem, was a friend and patron of Martial's (Shackleton Bailey 3:355). *Quadrantem*, the amount that here is translated as "a cent," is a quarter of an *as*, a low-value bronze coin. Since it doesn't make sense for someone to leave money to himself, Shackleton Bailey proposes that Crispus has spent all of his money before he dies (1:385n).

5.33.   Martial is threatening to satirize the lawyer if he learns which one is criticizing his verse.

5.34.   Martial writes several elegies for his little slave girl Erotion, whose shade he asks his dead parents to watch over in the underworld, so that she will not be frightened by Cerberus, the three-headed hound guarding Tartarus. She died six days short of her sixth birthday.

5.36.   Martial complains to his friend Faustinus about having been cheated by a man he flattered in the hope of reward, only to discover that the man had no sense of obligation to Martial in return. The humor lies in the implication that flattery creates a kind of contract between the flatterer and the flattered (Shackleton Bailey 1:387n).

5.42.   The flames are impious because they destroy the familial *lares*, the household gods here used to symbolize the family home (Howell, *Martial: Epigrams V* 128). The mistress is presumably despoiling the steward not by sleeping with him, but by demanding large sums of money that must come out of the estate of her lover. This poem, which argues that the only way to be sure to benefit from wealth is by giving it to friends and receiving their permanent gratitude, may be a graceful way to ask for money.

5.43.   Thais and Laecania are names used by Martial for prostitutes (Howell, *Martial: Epigrams V* 129).

5.45.   Martial implies that if Bassa were either young or beautiful, she wouldn't need to say so.

5.46.   Martial states that the sexual unwillingness of his slave Diadumenus is part of the attraction, so he beats the boy to make him resistant, then begs him for sex. The frequent beatings cause resentment, so he loses the boy's love, but the begging makes the boy aware of his power, so he ceases to fear Martial as well. Diadumenus is also mentioned in 3.65 and 6.34 and may be one of Martial's actual slaves (Shackleton Bailey 3:352).

5.47.  Philo's boast that he never dines at home suggests that he is much in demand as a dinner guest, but Martial implies that it actually means he can't afford to feed himself.

5.52.  The boasting of Postumus about his own generosity is bad form, as was Fabulla's boasting about her youth, beauty, and wealth in 1.64.

5.53.  Martial often puts down those who write on melodramatic mythological subjects. Here he suggests that Bassus has no understanding of Medea (who killed her own children and her husband's new bride as revenge for his abandonment of her), Thyestes (who was tricked into eating his own children by his brother Atreus), Niobe (who turned to stone from grief after all of her fourteen children were slaughtered by Apollo and Diana), or Andromache (whose husband was killed by Achilles and her baby son by the Greek army at Troy). Instead, Martial suggests more fitting subjects: Deucalion (one of the two survivors of a flood that killed the rest of humanity) or Phaethon (killed by a lightning bolt after nearly burning up the world while driving the chariot of the sun). Martial is slyly suggesting that flood and fire are appropriate subjects because the writing deserved to be washed out or burned (Shackleton Bailey 1:402n).

5.57.  Shackleton Bailey notes that boy slaves who were favorites of their master might be called "my lord" by him as a sign of their power over his heart (1:405n).

5.58.  Parthia and Armenia, both traditional enemies of Rome, were very far off, as well. Priam, the king of Troy, and Nestor, the king of Pylos, in *The Iliad* were both exemplars of men who had reached advanced age; the tomorrow in which Postumus will live has been postponed so long that it is now as old as they are.

5.59.  Martial suggests that his modest gift of earthenware is meant to remove any obligation from Stella to give expensive gifts in return. Lucius Arruntius Stella, himself a poet, was a friend and patron of Martial (Howell, *Martial: Epigrams V* 142).

5.64.  Howell notes that Falernian was an excellent and expensive wine, and cooling it with snow in summer would also be an expensive luxury. Romans typically perfumed their hair with scented oils and wore floral garlands on their heads at drinking parties. Slaves named Callistus and Alcimus appear also in 8.67 and 1.88 as Martial's own slaves, though in 1.88 Alcimus is said to have died. The Mausolea most likely included the tombs of Augustus and Julius Caesar (both deified after their deaths), which Martial could probably have seen from his apartment on the Quirinal hill (Howell, *Martial: Epigrams V* 147–48).

5.66. "Farewell forever" was the typical salutation to the dead (Shackleton Bailey 1:413n). By never greeting Martial first, Pontilianus would be treating him as a social inferior (Howell, *Martial: Epigrams V* 150).

5.68. Shackleton Bailey guesses that this is not a compliment to Lesbia, but a satirical suggestion that she bleaches her hair too much (1:413n). To have lighter hair than the true blondes would look phony. Lesbia was the name Catullus gave to the woman he loved; Martial tends to use the name in epigrams of a sexual nature (Howell, *Martial: Epigrams V* 151).

5.73. Martial uses the name Theodorus, meaning "God's gift" (Howell, *Martial: Epigrams V* 155), for a bad poet in 11.93, and writes a similar excuse for not sending free copies of his books to another poet, Pontilianus, in 7.3.

5.74. Howell notes that Pompey the Great's older son was killed in Asia Minor, his younger son in Spain, and himself in Egypt (Libya is here used to suggest Africa). His family was thus spread among the three known continents, though there is some question about whether Pompey himself was buried at all (*Martial: Epigrams V* 155–56).

5.75. The *Lex Iulia de adulteriis coercendis*, a law originated by Augustus to discourage adultery, was revived by Domitian in 85 CE (Howell, *Martial: Epigrams V* 156).

5.76. Howell notes that Mithridates VI of Pontus fought the Romans in three wars in the first century BCE. Pliny recounts that Mithridates took poison in small doses to build up an immunity to it, since eastern rulers often had to fear poison from rivals or members of their own families (cited in Howell, *Martial: Epigrams V* 156). Martial is probably making fun of Cinna not for being poor, but for being miserly (156).

5.79. Zoilus is using sweating as an excuse to show off his extensive wardrobe of fancy dinner suits. A *synthesis* is a matching tunic and loose, sleeveless cloak, usually worn at dinner parties (Howell, *Martial: Epigrams V* 161). Martial jokes that he himself doesn't sweat at the party of Zoilus because he doesn't have a second suit to change into.

5.81. The idea that "the rich get richer" would have special relevance in Rome, where people regularly gave lavish gifts to the wealthy in hope of legacies or other benefits from them.

5.82. The Greek name Gaurus means "pompous," which is relevant in this epigram (Howell, *Martial: Epigrams V* 163). He boasts of the large sums he will give Martial, but then gives nothing at all.

5.83. Howell notes that the name Dindymus comes from a mountain associated with the goddess Cybele, known for having eunuchs as her priests. Martial uses it of boys in erotic contexts (*Martial: Epigrams V* 164). Because the name is Greek, it would likely be the name of a slave. Martial frequently returns to the theme of the erotic stimulus provided by reluctance in a lover.

# Book Six

6.6. Martial implies that Paula, the wife or mistress of Lupercus, loves not only all three actors, but a fourth in a nonspeaking role. The Greek term means "walker-on" (Shackleton Bailey 2:5n).

6.12. As in 2.20, Martial's joke here is based on the idea that once you buy something, it is considered to be yours.

6.14. Martial implies that such a person does not exist (Shackleton Bailey 2:11n).

6.15. *Phaethontea* refers to the sisters of Phaethon, who were transformed into poplar trees that wept the sap that became amber. Amber that contained trapped insects was more valuable than clear amber. I wish to thank an anonymous reviewer of this manuscript for pointing out that the amber drop symbolizes an epigram itself, which makes common objects precious by means of a rich setting.

6.16. The god Priapus, guardian of gardens, was portrayed with a huge penis and a sickle, and was supposed to keep thieves away with the threat of castration (for men) or rape: oral rape for men, vaginal for women, or anal for boys (Richlin, *Garden of Priapus* 121). Martial tells the statue of Priapus that guards his small orchard to keep away the adult thieves, but allow in boys and long-haired girls, presumably not to be kind, but to enable Martial to rape or sodomize them himself.

6.17. Shackleton Bailey points out that the Greek freedman Cinnamus wishes to change his name to a Roman name, Cinna, to hide his slave origins. Martial calls the idea barbarous (punning on the Greek word meaning "foreigner") and suggests that if Cinnamus had originally had the name Furius, it ought to be shortened to *Fur*, Latin for "thief" (Shackleton Bailey 2:13n).

6.18. This poem seems to be intended to comfort Terentius Priscus, a Spanish friend and patron of Martial's (Shackleton Bailey 3:385), for the death of his relative Saloninus (3:380–81).

6.20. Martial frequently portrays himself as asking for loans from reluctant patrons. Here he implies that the loan isn't worth the wait that Phoebus puts him through.

6.22. The *lex Iulia* was a recently revived law to punish adultery.

6.23. Lesbia, the pseudonym used by Catullus for his mistress, is a name Martial often uses for women of loose morals. Here he implies that her imperious commands are off-putting in themselves and are further contradicted by her ugly face.

6.24. Men usually wore togas only on formal occasions, not on holidays such as the Saturnalia.

6.30. The sum Martial asked to borrow would be a small one to a rich man, though it was about five times the annual salary of a Roman legionary (a fact for which I am indebted to an anonymous reviewer). Clearly, Martial needed it urgently. Given when it is no longer needed, it creates no gratitude toward the giver.

6.33. Presumably Sabellus has had to marry to make up for his financial losses.

6.34. Martial alludes to poems 5 and 7 of Catullus, in which Catullus proposes to add up the thousands of kisses he begs from Lesbia. Catullus, however, also proposed to muddle the total, a fact that Martial ignores (as an anonymous reviewer pointed out).

6.36. Martial often makes fun of people who have exaggerated physical characteristics.

6.40. Lycoris and Glycera are both names that Martial often uses for prostitutes.

6.41. The unnamed poet in question has a sore throat and yet tries to recite anyway.

6.45. This epigram alludes to the *lex Iulia*, meant to punish adultery. Laetoria (who was an adulteress while she was single) will behave even worse when she herself is married and therefore safe from having her adultery exposed by becoming pregnant.

6.46. Shackleton Bailey mentions that "to do a great thing" could mean "to make a lot of money," but he dismisses that possibility as being irrelevant, preferring Birt's suggestion that the horses are defecating (Shackleton Bailey 2:36n). The driver, however, could be making a lot of money by losing deliberately, if he were paid to throw the race. The lashing of the horses could be for show, if the charioteer did other things to make it hard for the horses to run.

6.48. Pomponius is presumably an orator or advocate whose fine dinners ensure a devoted crowd of clients to shout his praise.

6.50. Martial implies that Telesinus is earning money through his sexual services to effeminate men.

6.51. Martial jokes that he will snub Lupercus for not inviting him to dinner, implying that even if Lupercus begs and pleads . . . Martial will come.

6.52. Like 5.34, this poem seems to be about one of Martial's own slaves, who died as a child. His epitaphs for dead child slaves show Martial at his most tender.

6.53. Faustinus was a patron and friend of Martial's and is mentioned in many other epigrams of his (Shackleton Bailey 3:355). The tendency of doctors to kill rather than cure is one of Martial's standard jokes, here exaggerated for effect so that even a dream of the doctor can be deadly.

6.55. Martial is implying both that Coracinus is effeminate for his over-use of perfume and that he is covering up other odors with it, such as those from performing oral sex. The mythical phoenix, a bird that was the only one of its kind, would be reborn from the ashes after burning itself on a nest of spices.

6.56. Martial hints that the gossip accuses Charidemus of something even more shameful than being sodomized, presumably performing oral sex.

6.57. Though wigs were available to cover baldness, Phoebus resorts to painting curls on his head with ointment.

6.59. Martial frequently attacks those who like to show off their extensive wardrobes unnecessarily, contrasting their abundance with his own more limited wardrobe.

6.60. Martial implies that he is as happy to arouse a negative reaction as a positive one with his poems. If the poems annoy some, the satire must be working.

6.62. This poem satirizes fortune hunters who ingratiate themselves with the rich and childless in the hope of inheriting their fortunes. Here Martial makes the practice even more repellent by portraying the fortune hunter as a vulture feeding on the fresh corpse of the son.

6.66. Martial implies that auctioneers had such a poor reputation that even a common whore is reluctant to kiss one. When the auctioneer kisses the whore to prove that she is clean, he lowers her value more.

6.79. When Lupus remains depressed despite his good fortune, Martial suggests, he is insulting the goddess who gave him good luck.

6.82. Batavians were a barbarian tribe living in what is now Holland (Shackleton Bailey 3:343). Martial suggests that, as foreigners, they wouldn't get Martial's jokes. This epigram illustrates both Martial's self-deprecatory humor and his skill at gracefully asking for favors from patrons.

6.84. This poem puns on two meanings of *sanus*. Though Philippus is sound of body, Martial implies that he is not sound of mind to insist on being carried on a litter (Shackleton Bailey 2:67n).

6.86. Setine wine was of high quality. Martial implies that his doctors are telling him not to drink for the sake of his health. Midas is symbolic both of great wealth and of foolishness, since once he got his wish to be able to turn all he touched to gold, he was unable to eat or drink. The poem lists harvests from Libya (one of the breadbaskets of the Roman Empire) and the Tagus and Hermus, gold-bearing rivers in Hispania (Shackleton Bailey 3:384) and Lydia (3:358) respectively, as symbols of the wealth that Martial would not trade for the pleasures of wine.

6.90. Gellia's moderation in adultery is offset by the fact that she is a bigamist.

6.91. Martial says elsewhere that Zoilus is a fellator (Shackleton Bailey 2:71n). Martial's congratulations are ironic, because the poem implies that Zoilus performs even more shameful acts than adultery.

# Book Seven

7.3. This epigram is addressed to Pontilianus. Martial refers to the common practice of exchanging books with other writers in 5.73 as well.

7.4. Scholars and poets were noted for their paleness, but in 1.77 Martial alludes to the idea that pallor can be caused by performing cunnilingus. Oppianus claims to be a poet in order to avoid the imputation that he performs cunnilingus (Shackleton Bailey 2:76–77n.). Castricus was a poet friend of Martial's (3:347).

7.9. Cascellius has the intelligence and talent to be a lawyer, but lacks the public speaking skills (Shackleton Bailey 2:81n).

7.11. Aulus Pudens was a friend of Martial's and is mentioned in many of his epigrams (Shackleton Bailey 3:378). The poem implies that Pudens wants Martial to emend the books in his own hand to increase their value (2:82n).

7.13. Shackleton Bailey notes that sulfurous fumes from the springs at Tibur were reported to have the ability to bleach ivory (2:84n). Galán Vioque points out that Tibur could be called "the hills of Hercules" because of the temple to Hercules found there (116). Lycoris would not be literally black, but her skin would be darker than it was before she left, presumably because exposing her skin to the air also exposed it to the sun.

7.14. The Aulus of this poem is the same Aulus Pudens mentioned in 7.11 (Shackleton Bailey 3:378). Martial alludes to poem 3 of Catullus, mourning the death of his mistress Lesbia's pet sparrow, as well as to a poem written by Martial's patron Stella in imitation of that poem, about the death of the pet black dove of his mistress Ianthis. Whereas Catullus had used erotic language to describe Lesbia's relation to her pet bird, Martial makes the sexual relationship with the "pet" literal. The overblown language of the lament is deliberately undercut by the discovery that the pet the girlfriend has lost is a young male slave with an oversized penis. Galán Vioque points out that the manuscript reads *denos*, not *senos*, which would make the boy's age twenty instead of twelve (127). One can assume either that "boy" is used ironically of one who is still developing physically at twenty or that the twelve-year-old is outrageously precocious in his development. I have chosen to go with the assumption of precocity, but either assumption is funny in its absurdity.

7.16. Marcus Aquilius Regulus was a famous advocate and patron of Martial, who addressed several epigrams to him (Shackleton Bailey 3:379). Patrons usually gave their clients gifts, loans, or dinner invitations rather than cash payments, affording the appearance of friendship to what was often a dependent relationship. Martial humorously offers to sell the gifts of Regulus back to their donor to make some ready cash.

7.18. Symmachus is a name Martial also uses in 5.9 for a doctor. The belief that a fart could kill a person if not released was common. It is mentioned, for instance, in a Greek epigram by Nicarchus in *The Greek Anthology* (11:395).

7.19. The fragment of wood described in this epigram supposedly once formed part of the keel of the Argo, the first ship to sail the sea, which was therefore "unknown" before (Galán Vioque 153). Jason and his crew, in order to retrieve the Golden Fleece, had to sail between the Cyanean Rocks, which clashed together to crush anything that came between them, and into the Black Sea (here called the Scythian Sea because the land of Scythia bordered it on the northeast). This scrap of keel may have been owned by one of Martial's wealthy patrons and praise of it would therefore be intended as indirect praise of the patron.

7.21. Argentaria Polla, the widow of the poet Lucan (Shackleton Bailey 3:377), was one of Martial's early patrons (1:1). Lucan had been forced to commit suicide by Emperor Nero (3:364).

7.25. Martial here argues in favor of caustic wit in epigrams, attacking an unnamed rival whose epigrams lack that quality. Galán Vioque notes that Romans used white lead carbonate powder to lighten their complexions (186), and that the Chian fig "has a special taste, like a mixture of wine and salt" (190).

7.30. This satirical attack is both xenophobic and misogynistic in targeting a Roman woman who sleeps with foreigners of any race, but not with her own kind. The fact that she is a Roman citizen is withheld until the penultimate line for added impact. Galán Vioque points out that Parthians, Germans, and Dacians were noted enemies of Rome; that all of the nationalities mentioned were from very distant parts of the empire; that Memphis and the Pharos lighthouse were in Egypt; and that circumcision was looked down on by Romans. The fact that the Scythian is mounted suggests sex in which the woman is "riding" the man (216–19).

7.39. Martial often refers to the tediousness of paying morning calls on patrons. Here Caelius has found a plausible excuse for avoiding the visits by faking gout, but he fakes it so well that soon he has the disease for real.

7.43. As in 6.20, Martial complains about a patron who will neither grant a request nor refuse it, keeping Martial in suspense.

7.46. Thalia is the Muse of comedy, so Priscus is presumably trying to compete with Martial in writing witty epigrams. But Martial points out that poor men like himself would rather have the present than the poem.

7.48. Martial is making fun of a host who departs from the usual custom of having tables for his guests. Instead, the dishes are carried around by pages. Martial complains that the dishes come by so fast that diners can't grab them.

7.62. Galán Vioque notes that for a man to have sex with an adult male slave was less acceptable than to do so with a boy, but not embarrassing so long as the slave took the passive role. The preference of Hamillus for adult slaves is suspicious and inspires Martial's conclusion that Hamillus buggers the slaves in public to hide his taking the passive role in private (361–62).

7.70. Galán Vioque points out that Martial uses the active form of the verb meaning "to fuck," implying that Philaenis, a lesbian, takes the masculine role in sex. *Amica* means both "female friend" and "female lover" (402–3).

7.75. The figure of the lecherous old woman who has to pay for sex is a frequent target of Martial's. Here she deludes herself that someone would be willing to sleep with her for free. In Latin, the punch line says "you want to give and not to give," punning on two meanings of *dare*: "to offer oneself sexually" and "to offer money."

7.76. Galán Vioque observes that dinner parties, porticoes, and theaters were places that people would go to pick up lovers (432). The implication is that Philomusus may provide sexual pleasure or entertainment, but is not loved.

7.77. Copies of books were expensive to make, and though Martial might offer them for free to generous patrons, he implies that Tucca wants to make money by reselling them.

7.78. Saxetanum was a town in southern Spain known for producing salted fish; *lacerti* were small fish (Shackleton Bailey 2:141n). One might expect a man who eats the tail of a small salted fish, accompanied by oiled beans if he is dining well, to be poor, yet Papylus sends luxury foods as gifts to others. He is being satirized as the worst sort of miser, who denies himself any pleasures while sending expensive gifts to others in the hope of receiving legacies or gifts from them. Shackleton Bailey explains that to "indulge one's Genius" means to enjoy oneself, which Papylus is incapable of doing (2:141n).

7.79. Galán Vioque points out that "consular" usually referred to something from the Republican period, which would have made the wine quite old. Romans valued old wines highly, and tended to look down on new wines. The wine's vintage was indicated by naming who was consul when it was produced (440–41). Martial is here using "consular" to mean "wine of a consul." There had been three consuls named Priscus not long before this book was published in 92 CE (Shackleton Bailey 2:143n). Marcus Severus was a friend of Martial's (3:382).

7.81. Lausus is a friend of Martial's (Shackleton Bailey 3:363). Martial frequently feels a need to defend himself against the criticism that his work is uneven, as he does also in 1.16. In 7.90, on the other hand, he points out that consistency is not always a virtue.

7.83. Galán Vioque says that the Greek name Eutrapelus means "nimble," but that this barber seems to be inordinately slow (453–54). An alternate explanation is that Lupercus is so hairy that the barber can't keep up with his beard's growth. The epigram literally says that the barber "paints" the cheeks of Lupercus, which could mean applying makeup (454), but could also refer to the ruddiness created by shaving.

7.85. Martial here, as in 7.81, refers to the difficulty of maintaining consistently high quality in a book of epigrams.

7.89. Domitius Appolinaris was a friend and patron of Martial (Shackleton Bailey 3:340), who here sends him a rose garland (customarily worn at banquets) as a gift. The poem expresses a wish for the long life of his patron (Galán Vioque 480).

7.90. This poem is addressed to Creticus, not mentioned elsewhere in Martial. Galán Vioque notes that *creticus* is the name of an unequal metrical foot, so the name may be intended as a pun (482).

7.91. The Juvenal addressed here was probably the satirist Decimus Junius Juvenalis, a friend of Martial's (Shackleton Bailey 3:361). Galán Vioque notes that nuts were a common token gift for Saturnalia. Martial apologizes for the smallness of the gift by joking that the rest of the nuts from his farm were used by the orchard's guardian god, Priapus, to bribe girls into having sex with him (484–85).

7.92. Martial is satirizing a patron who is all talk, no action. Baccara, to spare Martial's dignity, offers to give him financial help whenever he needs it without Martial's having to ask for it. Yet faced with several clear examples of Martial's financial need, Baccara does nothing. Martial wishes a baleful star to strike Baccara dumb as fitting punishment for his empty words of support.

7.94. The mouth of Papylus smells so bad from performing oral sex that anything that comes near it is tainted by his smell. Garum, a fish sauce made from fermented carp entrails and gills, was widely used in Roman cooking and noted for its offensive odor (Galán Vioque 495–96).

## Book Eight

8.1. As in book 5, Martial is flattering Emperor Domitian by complying with his expressed preference for moral writing. Martial also alludes here to Domitian's veneration of Pallas Minerva, symbolizing wisdom, as opposed to sex, symbolized by Venus.

8.5. Macer's gifts to his mistresses have impoverished him to the point that he no longer has the minimum qualification for knighthood of owning four hundred thousand sesterces (Galán Vioque 372). Senators, knights, and magistrates had the right to wear a gold ring (Shackleton Bailey 2:164n). *Macer* means "lean, meager," so the name fits the character.

8.10. Tyrian purple was the most expensive color to produce.

8.12. Martial addresses more than one Priscus in his poems, so the identity of this one cannot be established (Shackleton Bailey 3:378), but it is probably one of his friends.

8.13. Martial implies that he wanted a foolish slave who would be tractable, but got one that was clever and therefore less desirable.

8.14. Boreas, the North Wind, is usually portrayed as being fierce and tough. Martial jokes that his unnamed host's greenhouses would be more comfortable than his guest rooms.

8.16. Cyperus, who was a baker for a long time, became an advocate, earning a lot of money, but spending even more. Martial's joke is that turning bread back into flour would make something valuable into something worth much less, just as Cyperus takes a lucrative job and then dissipates all his earnings (Shackleton Bailey 2:172n).

8.17. Martial here pretends that he has become a lawyer and has pled a case for Sextus, who underpays him when the case is lost. Martial hints that the facts of the case were so damning that it was better not to mention them (Shackleton Bailey 2:173n), implying that he blushed as a move to win sympathy.

8.18. Cerrinius is clearly a friend of Martial's and probably one of his patrons. Martial's praise of his unpublished epigrams and comparison of his modesty to Vergil's unwillingness to compete with Horace in writing odes or with Varius in writing tragedy are elaborate compliments and should not be taken as a sincere estimate of the epigrams' worth. Vergil's full name was Publius Vergilius Maro (Shackleton Bailey 3:389); Horace, who lived in Calabria (2:173n), had the full name of Quintus Horatius Flaccus (3:355); Lucius Varius Rufus was a writer of tragedies during the time of Augustus (3:388). Buskins (*cothurni* in Latin) were boots worn by actors in tragedies and therefore an allusion to tragedy in general.

8.19. Because so many rich men would plead poverty to avoid financial obligations, Cinna hopes that by harping on his poverty he can be taken for a rich man, but his claimed poverty is no pretense (Shackleton Bailey 2:174n).

8.20. Martial loves the paradox by which someone can have a quality and its opposite at the same time. Here Varus is unwise to write so much bad poetry, but wise not to recite it in public. The name Varus means "contrary" in Latin, which suits such a contradictory character.

8.22. Wild boar would be a rarer, more expensive delicacy than pork; Martial implies that he can tell the difference between the two (Shackleton Bailey 2:175n), that he is no hybrid and neither is the pig.

8.23. The name Rusticus means "provincial, boorish" in Latin and therefore suits someone who questions his host's behavior in a foolish way.

8.25.   On the surface, Martial appears to be offering to comfort Oppianus often when he becomes ill, but the offer contains the implied hope that Oppianus will be ill often (Shackleton Bailey 2:177n). Martial may also intend to gloat when he visits.

8.27.   Gaurus is one of many cases Martial mentions of rich men beset by legacy hunters, but he appears to be unaware of his visitors' motives.

8.29.   Martial suggests that no matter how short the individual poems may be, one still needs enough of them to fill a book and the book will still be as long as if the poems were long ones. He often seems to be responding defensively to readers who tell him that they like his shortest poems best.

8.31.   Howell notes that Martial had asked for and received the Right of Three Children (*ius trium liberorum*) from Emperor Titus, and the grant was renewed under Domitian. The rights included the right to receive legacies (15–16). Since Martial does not seem to have married, the rights would have been a significant coup for him, but he makes fun of married men who seek the same privilege.

8.35.   Martial plays on the irony of the couple's not getting along despite being perfectly matched in awfulness.

8.40.   Images of Priapus, the fertility god, were placed in gardens to guard them from theft. Here the image guarding a grove intended for fire-wood is itself made of wood and therefore may be burned if it fails to protect the grove (Shackleton Bailey 2:191n).

8.41.   The Faustinus mentioned in this poem is the same friend and patron of Martial's mentioned in several other poems (Shackleton Bailey 3:355). The gift exchange would have been during the Saturnalia, a seven-day festival that began on December 17 (3:381).

8.43.   Martial implies that Fabius and Chrestilla tend to do away with their spouses soon after the wedding, presumably to inherit the spouse's money. With poetic justice, he suggests that they should marry one another, so that both will be carried off at the same time by Libitina, the goddess of burials.

8.47.   Martial seems to be satirizing an unduly elaborate treatment of facial hair.

8.51.   Shackleton Bailey observes that any lover might see more in the beloved than is there, but the phrase "loves more than he sees" is literally true for a blind man (2:201n).

8.54.   Though Shackleton Bailey emends *vilissima* to *durissima* and *magis* to *minus*, the unemended epigram makes sense if you assume that Martial is lamenting that a beautiful woman should be utterly shameless. The name he gives the woman, Catulla, would evoke for many readers the Lesbia of Catullus, just such a shameless beauty.

8.56. This sort of over-the-top praise of Domitian, a notably bad emperor, has earned Martial the disapproval of many, who assume that he is flattering the emperor to gain perks from him. In some poems Martial asks for specific benefits, but in many, as here, the praise is not tied to any particular request. By linking Domitian's generosity to the people's love, however, Martial is subtly encouraging more generosity. Spisak points out that such praise poems encourage behavior helpful to the community (54) by appealing to the desire of the rich and powerful to acquire a good reputation and to maintain it after their death (60).

8.60. The Palatine Colossus, originally a statue of Nero erected by his Golden House, was moved by Vespasian to the Via Sacra and converted into a statue of the Sun God, with a diadem of rays (Shackleton Bailey 1:13n). Martial frequently exaggerates physical features for humorous effect, and a towering woman is a funnier image than a giant man.

8.61. Like many of Martial's other poems about his Nomentan farm, this one emphasizes the nuisances, rather than the pleasures, of ownership. Marcus Severus, to whom the poem is addressed, was a literary man and Martial's friend (Shackleton Bailey 3:382). The bosses and cedar oil would have adorned Martial's books, not Martial himself.

8.62. Papyrus was expensive, and Martial is satirizing a scrimping poet who tries to reuse old scrolls by writing on their backs. Apollo's turning his back on Picens implies that the poet has no inspiration.

8.69. Martial often mentions earlier Latin poets with respect, especially Catullus, Vergil, Ovid, Horace, and Marsus, but he clearly found it annoying that earlier poets were valued far above living poets, such as himself.

8.76. Gallicus asks for truth and gets it, but not the "truth" he wanted. Rich patrons must often have asked Martial's opinion on their writing and speaking abilities. In this epigram about an invented character, Martial can give the blunt answer he might have hesitated to give to an actual patron.

8.77. Martial's friend Liber was a charioteer (Shackleton Bailey 3:363). Falernian is Martial's usual choice to signify an excellent, expensive wine. The Assyrian cardamom oil is another luxury, which people would use to scent their hair at banquets.

8.79. Porticoes were covered walkways that functioned as popular meeting places, providing shelter from sun or rain. By surrounding herself with old and ugly friends, Fabulla makes herself look young and beautiful by comparison.

## Book Nine

9.4. There are many possible reasons that Aeschylus might want to buy Galla's silence, all of them embarrassing, such as impotence or fetishes. Leaving the possibilities open to the reader's imagination makes them seem even more lurid than they would be if stated.

9.6. According to Henriksén, the pseudonym Afer, meaning "African," may have been chosen because of its connection to Libya (42). Afer is clearly a patron, and as his client, the poet would be expected to visit him after his return. By remaining unavailable, the patron is causing considerable trouble to the client, who must keep returning. The final *vale* is a pun, meaning not only "goodbye," but also "get lost," and, because of its ritual use at funerals, "drop dead" (43).

9.8. Bithynicus has clearly been legacy hunting by giving six thousand sesterces a year to Fabius, only to learn that Fabius has died penniless. Martial advises him to look on the bright side: he won't have to keep giving six thousand a year.

9.9. Cantharus makes himself an unwelcome dinner guest by his out-spoken abuse and bad manners. Martial warns him that he is unlikely to be invited to dinner if he doesn't change his ways. Henriksén points out that the Greek name Cantharus is derived from the name of a drinking cup associated with Bacchus, the god of wine, and that drunkenness therefore may be the source of the character's bad behavior (51). There is a complex pun in the term *liber*, which means "a free man," "free speaking," and "one of the names of Bacchus, the god of wine" (52). If Cantharus wants to eat and drink at his patron's expense, he has to remember that he is dependent on the patron and cannot say whatever he wants.

9.10. The scenario in which a woman is eager to marry and a man isn't comes up frequently in Martial's epigrams. Here, the implication is that Paula is undesirable for an unnamed reason. Martial frequently writes about old women wanting to marry younger men, who would be tempted to marry them only for their money.

9.14. Parasites who constantly seek dinner invitations from people known for their lavish banquets are a common target of Martial's. Martial frequently mentions boar, mullet, sow's udder, and oysters as expensive and desirable dishes.

9.15. A typical tomb inscription, *Chloe feci* means "I, Chloe, put up [this tomb]," but could also mean "I, Chloe, did it" (Shackleton Bailey 2:244n).

9.19. Shackleton Bailey notes that "three hundred verses" implies just "a large number" (2:247n). Like the dinner seeker of 9.14, Sabellus uses flattery to deflect attention from what he is really after, a lavish meal. Ironically, as Hendriksén observes, Martial himself had written a rather long poem, 6.42, in praise of the baths of Claudius Etruscus (86).

9.21. Pompeius Auctus was a legal expert and an admirer of Martial's work (Shackleton Bailey 3:377). He is being asked to determine which of the two men got the better end of the exchange. Martial is here punning on the erotic symbolism of "plowing" in the closeness of *amat* (he loves) to *arat* (he plows).

9.25. Hyllus is clearly not just any page, but Afer's catamite, whom he watches jealously when others show attention to him. A Gorgon was a monster who turned to stone anyone who looked at her. Hylas was a boy loved by Hercules (Alcides), and Ganymede was a boy loved by Jupiter. Oedipus blinded himself after discovering his wife was actually his mother, and Phineus was a blind seer in the story of Jason and the Argonauts. When Martial mentions looking at gods, right after mentioning temples, he means the statues of gods that would be in the temples (Henriksén 108).

9.32. Martial expresses a preference for a common prostitute over a grasping courtesan or stuck-up Roman woman (Henriksén 143). Burdigala, meaning "from Bordeaux," is the kind of rich but stupid provincial that Martial suggests such a woman will have to settle for. The prostitute is portrayed as walking around in a cloak, possibly wearing little or nothing under it. According to Henriksén, one denarius (equal to ten *asses*) was a reasonable fee for a prostitute, and two would not be expensive, especially if anything more than standard sex was involved (145–46).

9.33. Flaccus was a rich friend of Martial's, to whom many of his epigrams are addressed (Shackleton Bailey 3:355). Since people bathed naked, some ogling would have occurred (and Martial often implies that that is the case), but the applause is almost certainly an exaggeration for humorous effect. Henriksén notes that it cannot be an accident that the last names of Horace (Flaccus) and Vergil (Maro) appear together here (148–49). The applause mentioned may be an indirect compliment to the authors, but the sexual subtext clearly adds a note of satire, too.

9.40. The Tarpeian wreath was the prize in the Capitoline poetry contest (Shackleton Bailey 2:267n). Pharos is an island offshore from Alexandria in Egypt. Sabine women were renowned for their virtue. That a woman who is not a debased prostitute should volunteer to perform fellatio on her man if he returns safely is presented as a sign of her anxiety for his welfare, but also of her naïveté.

9.44. According to Shackleton Bailey, this poem concerns a statuette of Hercules owned by the poet Novius Vindex and written about by both Martial and Statius. The statuette was supposedly made by Lysippus for Alexander the Great (2:270n). By pretending to think it was made instead by Phidias, whom Martial consistently mentions as one of the greatest Greek artists (Henriksén 200), Martial is complimenting the statuette. For a poet not to know Greek would have been extremely embarrassing (199). Here Martial pretends ignorance partly to turn the joke on himself and partly to set up the compliment.

9.50. Martial compares his poems to two famous bronze statuettes that were acknowledged masterpieces: Brutus' boy, a statuette by Strongylion that was a favorite of Brutus the Tyrannicide, and Langon, a statuette of a boy by Lyciscus (Henriksén 222–23). The Greek name Gaurus means "haughty, disdainful" (219), which fits the attitude of the poet described in this epigram.

9.52. Quintus Ovidius, one of Martial's best friends, had a farm next to his in Nomentum. Martial alludes to the custom of using a white pebble to mark an especially fortunate day on the calendar (Henriksén 229).

9.53. This poem is also addressed to Quintus Ovidius, a close friend of Martial's who is mentioned in 9.52 and in several other poems (Shackleton Bailey 3:372). He was a close enough friend that he would not be offended by the joking reference to his imperiousness or the suggestion that he give Martial a gift instead of receiving one from him.

9.60. Henriksén notes that floral garlands were common gifts between friends; the recipient, Caesius Sabinus, was mentioned as well in several other epigrams of Martial's. Paestum, Praeneste, and Campania were all famous for their roses, and Tusculum for its violets, whereas Martial frequently complains of the meager output of his farm at Nomentum. Nevertheless, he suggests that the gift will seem more personal if Sabinus thinks the flowers come from his own garden than if they were bought from a more prestigious source (256–57).

9.62. Henriksén comments that Tyrian purple dye was very expensive, so purple garments were often worn to show off one's wealth. The dye, however, also had a strong odor, which is here used to mask the nasty smell of Philaenis herself, possibly from incontinence (268–69).

9.63. There are several possible meanings of "fed by a cock" in this epigram. Martial suggests that Phoebus is invited to dinner by effeminate men in return for participating in sex with them. He is thus fed by his own cock, but may also, as Henriksén notes, be performing fellatio or being buggered, which were considered unclean, or buggering adult men, which was also looked down on (270).

9.66. As in his epigram 8.31, Martial is making fun of married men who petition Caesar for the Right of Three Children, when they should be able to beget children on their own. Martial implies that such a man must be impotent.

9.67. The "boy way" is anal intercourse; the next thing he asks for is fellatio, which was considered an act that defiled those who performed it. Since the girl is still pure as far as Martial is concerned, that implies that he does not follow through because of the condition she demands. A. E. Housman suggested that the girl demands that Martial perform oral sex on her in return; whereas Martial finds the condition to be outrageous and refuses, he implies that Aeschylus would not refuse it (cited in Henriksén 282).

9.69. Though the epigram is posed as a riddle, Henriksén suggests that the first line gives the answer to the second: that the cock of the sodomizer will be fouled by shit (290).

9.74. Henriksén notes that in epigram 6.85 Martial had stated that Camonius Rufus of Bononia (now Bologna) was a friend of his and knew many of his poems by heart. That poem mourned the early death of his friend in Cappadocia (305). In this epigram Martial alludes to the only portrait of his friend being from childhood, suggesting that the father of Camonius had avoided having a portrait made before the son left, either because it would distress him to be reminded of his son's absence or because he had a superstitious fear that the speechless image might foreshadow the speechlessness of death. The Roman custom of preserving busts of ancestors might reinforce the association of portraits with death.

9.78. The suggestion is that Galla poisoned her first seven husbands, but has now married a poisoner who will do the same to her (Shackleton Bailey 2:301n).

9.80. Martial implies that the old woman is so desperate for a husband that she is willing to perform oral sex on him, and he is so desperate for money that he is willing to fuck an old woman.

9.81. Aulus Pudens was a friend of Martial's and is addressed often in his epigrams (Shackleton Bailey 3:378). Martial often writes poems defending his writing against critics of various sorts, as in 9.50.

9.82. As Shackleton Bailey notes, Martial here puns on two meanings of *perire*, which could mean both "to die" and "to be ruined" (2:304). Munna thinks his death is predicted and spends all of his money, only to learn that he has caused his own financial ruin.

9.83. All reading was done aloud, but Martial is here satirizing those who recited their poetry to others; while they are watching shows in the arena, they are at least not boring their listeners (Shackleton Bailey 2:304n).

9.85. The Atilius mentioned here may be Atilius Crescens, who is mentioned as a man of letters by Pliny (Henriksén 334). Paulus pretends to be ill to get out of hosting a dinner, but Martial complains to Atilius, another friend of Paulus, that though the illness is fake, the dinner is dead. An ill man might be expected to fast (as in "feed a cold, starve a fever"), but Paulus makes his guests fast instead.

9.87. The wine Martial says he is drinking, Opimian, was proverbial as being one of the best vintages, though Henriksén suggests that there was little, if any, Opimian left in Martial's day, because the vintage it signified dated from 121 BCE (342). Martial hints that Lupercus is trying to take advantage of Martial's drunkenness by getting Martial to put his seal on a legal document that may be something other than what Lupercus says it is. By sealing the flask instead, Martial is signaling that he has drunk enough for one night. The practice also prevents servants from stealing wine (Shackleton Bailey 2:308n).

9.88. Martial describes a frequent practice of sending gifts to wealthy people in the hope of getting legacies from them. Here he implies that after the will is written, the gifts stop, but he reminds Rufus that one can change one's will.

9.89. Lucius Arruntius Stella was a friend and patron of Martial's and is mentioned in a number of his epigrams (Shackleton Bailey 3:383). Here he seems to have required Martial, as a dinner guest, to improvise verses on the spot. When Martial complains that improvising is too difficult, he is told that the verses needn't be good ones.

9.91. This epigram is an elaborate compliment to Domitian, implying that Martial would rather be his guest than the guest of Jupiter himself. Henriksén argues that the epigram was probably written to commemorate the completion of Domitian's new dining room in 94 CE, but the poem does not necessarily imply that Martial was invited to dinner there (353–54).

9.96. In epigram 6.78, Martial mentions a doctor ordering a patient to stop drinking in order to save his eyesight. Here, the doctor, caught stealing a wine ladle, pretends that he is doing it to protect his patient's health.

9.100. Although three denarii is almost twice the normal dole for a client (Shackleton Bailey 2:319n), the duties that Martial is expected to perform in return are so onerous that he does not think the extra money to be worth the bother.

9.102. Martial frequently writes about loans of money from wealthy men to those with less money. According to Henriksén, though it was assumed that such loans would be repaid, Martial often takes the humorous position that the wealthy can afford to lose the money and that paying it back is therefore a sign of virtue (415). Here Martial makes fun of a lender who tries to make canceling a bad debt look like a generous gift; he suggests that a true gift would be to offer another loan, knowing it too would not be repaid (413).

## Book Ten

10.1. The tenth book is a revised and enlarged edition (Shackleton Bailey 2:325n). Martial often mentions readers who complain about the length of his poems or books.

10.8. As in many other epigrams of Martial's, the joke here is that old women want husbands, but that men would only marry an old woman if she were wealthy and likely to die soon.

10.9. Poetry of eleven syllables per line is hendecasyllabics, one of Martial's common forms. His most common form, elegiacs, is what he means by "poetry of eleven feet," because it is organized into alternating lines of dactylic hexameter (six feet) and dactylic pentameter (five feet). Martial's comparison of his own fame to the racehorse's is typical of his self-deprecating humor.

10.16. Martial suggests that the archery mishap was no accident, but meant to dispose of the wife while retaining her dowry.

10.21. Modestus and Claranus are clearly scholarly commentators on literary texts, and Sextus, by writing so obscurely, is out to stump them. Shackleton Bailey suggests that the books of Sextus need Apollo because "they are as obscure as Delphic oracles" (2:345n). The poet C. Helvius Cinna wrote his *Smyrna* in an elaborate style, full of obscure allusions that would need explication (3:348). Martial implies that only someone as wrongheaded as Sextus could consider Cinna a greater writer than Vergil.

10.22. White lead and medicinal pastes were used to treat various ailments, but Martial here claims to use them when he is healthy as a way of keeping his distance from one he would rather not kiss (the implication, as usual, is that the one he would avoid performs oral sex).

10.23. Marcus Antonius Primus of Tolosa (now Toulouse) was a friend of Martial's (Shackleton Bailey 3:340). Fifteen Olympiads equals seventy-five years (2:345n).

10.27. Shackleton Bailey points out that thirty sesterces is four to five times the normal dole (2:349n). The last line of the epigram says literally "Yet nobody thinks you were born, Diodorus" (2:349). Diodorus is a nouveau-riche nobody who thinks he is important because patricians attend his lavish parties.

10.29. Martial often mentions that the Kalends of March (March 1) is his birthday. It was also the day on which gifts were customarily given to women (Shackleton Bailey 2:346n). Martial expected a gift of a toga, but Sextilianus gives a dining outfit to his mistress instead.

10.31. Mullet were an expensive fish in ancient Rome, and the larger they were, the more expensive they were. Shackleton Bailey notes that Martial puns on two meanings of "dining well": Calliodorus dines lavishly, but his actions are morally repugnant (2:353n).

10.32. Caedicianus is mentioned four times by Martial as being a friend of his (Shackleton Bailey 3:344). Marcus Antonius Primus is also mentioned in 10.23.

10.39. Shackleton Bailey identifies the Brutus mentioned here as Lucius Junius Brutus (3:344), who became consul in 509 BCE. That would make Lesbia close to six hundred years old. Martial goes on to even greater absurdities for comic effect. Numa Pompilius (753–673 BCE) was the second king of Rome (after Romulus), and Prometheus was the creator of humankind, whom he molded from clay.

10.40. Friendships between a wife or mistress and a male concubine were often suspected of leading to infidelity precisely because the effeminacy of the male concubine would be good cover for an affair (Shackleton Bailey 2:363n).

10.43. Martial's joke has several meanings: first, that to lose one wife is lucky, but to lose seven of them is extraordinarily fortunate; second, that each wife would be bringing a dowry with her, so the death of each allows Phileros to acquire another dowry; and third, that no crop Phileros could grow on the land could possibly produce as much income as he gets from his wives' deaths. Sullivan notes that the Greek name Phileros means "fond of love," an appropriate name for one who had found it to be so lucrative (246).

10.44. Scotland was known as Caledonia to the Romans. Atropos, one of the three Fates, is the one who cuts the life thread. Quintus Ovidius, mentioned also in other epigrams such as 1.105, was a close friend who owned property near Martial's Nomentan farm.

10.45. Laurentum, a town on the coast of Latium, is the source of the boar (Shackleton Bailey 3:362). Vatican wine had a very low reputation (3:388).

10.47. Lucius Julius Martialis was Martial's closest friend, a lawyer who owned a small estate on the Janiculum, a hill across the Tiber from Rome (Sullivan 17). Martial desires the strength that would be appropriate for a gentleman, Shackleton Bailey observes, not for an athlete or laborer (2:368n). This poem is the most often translated of all of Martial's epigrams (Sullivan 50).

10.49. Opimian wine was an extremely old and famous vintage, dating from 121 BCE, when Opimius was consul (Shackleton Bailey 1:61n). Though there was probably not much left of it by Martial's day, he uses the term to denote excellent old wine. Sabine wine was cheap and young (2:371n).

10.52. Shackleton Bailey notes that the toga, which was worn on formal occasions by men, was also the garb that prostitutes and women convicted of adultery were forced to wear, by law, to differentiate them from respectable women. The eunuch Thelys is so effeminate that when he wears a toga he looks like an adulteress, not like a man. The joke may also imply that Thelys is guilty of having sexual contact with someone's wife, but isn't manly enough to be called an adulterer (2:375n).

10.53. Scorpus was a famous chariot racer who is mentioned repeatedly in Martial's epigrams (Shackleton Bailey 3:381). This poem is presented as if it were his epitaph.

10.54. Beautifully inlaid tables are frequently mentioned by Martial as a luxury item of the wealthy, doubtless to be displayed at dinner parties. Here he focuses on the absurdity of owning such tables and then covering them up with tablecloths.

10.59. In several other poems (such as 1.110 and 3.83) Martial complains about readers who like his short poems more than his longer ones. However, as he points out in 8.29, it is hard to fill a book if all of your poems are short ones. Here he compares a book to a meal, saying it can't all be tasty morsels; there needs to be some bread as well.

10.61. This poem is in the form of an epitaph, such as Martial might have written for the tomb of his slave girl Erotion, whose death he mourns in

5.34. He here invokes a blessing on anyone who will continue to make offerings to the spirit of the dead girl when he is no longer around to do so.

10.64. This poem is addressed to Argentaria Polla, the widow of the poet Lucan and one of Martial's earliest (Sullivan 317) and most generous patrons (102). The poem concerns her husband, author of an epic on the civil war between Julius Caesar and Pompey, and cites a line of his that may have come from an epigram that has not survived (Shackleton Bailey 2:383n). Helicon, a mountain in Greece associated with the Muses, is symbolic of poetic achievement, though "our Helicon" refers to the achievement of Latin poets. Literally, the last line of the Latin is "If I'm not even sodomized, Cotta, what am I doing here?" (2:383).

10.65. The Tagus is a river in Spain, a tributary of which, the Tagonius, flowed near Martial's home of Bilbilis (Sullivan 177). Corinth is in Greece. Martial claims to be descended from the Celts and Iberians who populated northeastern Spain. Iberians were noted for hairiness (172). *Silia* is Shackleton Bailey's suggested replacement for *filia* in the text; he assumes that it refers to a loud-voiced woman (2:385n).

10.66. Martial appears to be writing about the same boy, though unnamed, in epigram 12.64. Ganymede was a beautiful Trojan prince whom Jupiter abducted to be his cupbearer and catamite.

10.74. Shackleton Bailey notes that the plains of Apulia were famous for their wool (2:393n). Hybla was likewise noted for its honey, and much of the wheat consumed in Rome grew in the Nile region. Setia produced a famous wine, mentioned in many of Martial's epigrams. Scorpus was a famous charioteer whose death had already been the subject of Martial's elegy in 10.53, so it is not surprising that Martial does not want the wins of Scorpus at the price of an early death, but merely wants to be able to sleep late instead of spending his mornings visiting a series of patrons. The poem also looks forward to Martial's announcement at the end of book 10 that he plans to retire to his childhood home of Bilbilis in Hispania.

10.77. Martial suggests that the fever, which was also naughty, should have been a quartan fever, a malarial fever that returns every four days, instead of such a deadly fever that it killed Carus at once. The desire to see Carus under a doctor's care is not meant kindly, since Martial consistently portrays medical care as being a fate worse than death.

10.80. Eros, named after the Greek god of love, is probably a freedman, judging from his Greek name; it suits him because he desires everything he sees. The Saepta Julia ("the Enclosure") was located in the Campus Martius and contained shops (Shackleton Bailey 1:144–45n). Speckled murrine cups were carved from a semiprecious stone and were quite expensive. Fancy table-tops of citrus wood were also a luxury item, as were handsome slave boys.

10.81. Phyllis, whose Greek name suggests that she is a prostitute, takes on two customers at once by being sodomized by one while being fucked by the other.

10.84. This poem is addressed to Caedicianus, a friend of Martial's, possibly fictitious (Shackleton Bailey 3:344). Shackleton Bailey observes that there are two possible interpretations of the epigram: that the woman next to Afer at dinner is beautiful and he doesn't want to leave her, or that she is ugly and he doesn't want to go to bed with her (2:401n).

10.90. Ligeia is one of many lustful old women satirized by Martial. Depilation of pubic hair was considered attractive in young women.

10.91. Martial suggests that Almo is foolish to expect his wife Polla to have children when he himself is impotent and his male slaves are all eunuchs; if they weren't eunuchs, Martial implies, she would be having sex with them.

10.94. The "serpent of Numidia" is an allusion to the giant snake that guarded the golden apples of the Hesperides (Shackleton Bailey 2:411n). The gardens of Alcinous, described in *The Odyssey*, produced luscious fruit at all seasons. Martial jokes that the apples grown on his farm are too poor to steal or to give as a gift, so he has bought his gift of apples in the Subura, a bustling shopping district in Rome, not where they were actually grown.

10.95. Though the Latin does not include an equivalent for "What *did* you do?" the reader is meant to pick up the implication that the sex Galla had with her husband and lover did not include intercourse, and that she was cheating on both with someone else.

10.97. Myrrh and cassia (an aromatic bark resembling cinnamon) would be thrown on the pyre as it burned (Shackleton Bailey 2:413n).

10.100. Ladas was a famous Olympic runner (Shackleton Bailey 3:362). Martial frequently complains that others try to claim his own poems as theirs. Here he suggests that the difference between Martial's poems and the plagiarist's is obvious.

10.102. This poem is addressed to Lucius Stertinius Avitus, a friend and patron of Martial's (Shackleton Bailey 3:384). As in 10.100, Martial is attacking those who pass off the poems of others as their own.

## Book Eleven

11.13. Kay notes that in 82 or 83 CE, Paris, a celebrated and handsome pantomime, had been murdered on the orders of Emperor Domitian, who suspected him of having an affair with Domitian's wife, Domitia Longina. Domitian also executed those who openly mourned the death of Paris, so this epitaph could not be published until after Domitian's death in 96 CE (94). Literally, the poem states that all of the Venuses and Cupids are buried with Paris.

11.14.    Shackleton Bailey points out that "may the earth be light on you" was part of the standard prayer for the dead, but that plowing, digging, and carrying soil was hard work for a farmer and would have been particularly onerous for a man of small stature (3:319).

11.15.    This poem is addressed to Domitius Apollinaris, a friend and patron of Martial's (Shackleton Bailey 3:340). Cato the Younger was famous for his stringent moral standards, attributes that would be expected, as well, of his wife, since women were expected to be more prudish than men; the Sabine women were often mentioned as models of morality. Cosmus is mentioned often by Martial as a seller of perfumed ointments to be used on the hair. The word *mentula* was considered obscene, but Martial justifies it by pointing to the ancient precedent of Numa, the legendary second king of Rome. The winter holiday of the Saturnalia was a time of partying and license, so Martial uses the time of this book's publication to justify the inclusion of a larger number of obscene poems than usual (Kay 71). Sullivan argues that the greater incidence of obscene poems in the book is due to the replacement of Emperor Domitian by Nerva, whom Martial considered to be more tolerant because Nerva had written erotic elegies himself (47).

11.17.    The addressee, Caesius Sabinus, was a friend of Martial's (Shackleton Bailey 3:345).

11.19.    Galla is *diserta*, meaning "eloquent." Martial states that his cock often commits solecisms, implying that an eloquent wife would comment upon them. In short, he does not want a wife who would criticize either his grammar or his sexual conduct.

11.25.    Martial implies that the overactive sex life of Linus has left him impotent, but rather than give up sex entirely, Linus will resort to cunnilingus (always considered a shameful activity by the Romans).

11.28.    Hylas was a beautiful page whom Hercules loved. The name would therefore be appropriate for a catamite. Here Martial suggests that the madman's rape of the attractive catamite of Doctor Euctus is proof that the patient was actually sane.

11.29.    Lustful old women who have to buy sex from men are a favorite target of Martial's. Kay notes that Setine land was not far from Rome and was famous for producing excellent wine (136). The scenario described here is probably invented by Martial, like the scenarios in which he claims to have a wife.

11.30.  When Zoilus says that lawyers and poets have bad breath, he seems to imply that it is acquired by speaking at length (Shackleton Bailey 3:29n). Martial returns the insult by implying that Zoilus has bad breath from performing fellatio.

11.34.  The mystery of why Aper would buy an old hovel is solved when one hears that it is next to a splendid estate and that Aper expects to be invited to dine there.

11.35.  "Three hundred" is a typical exaggeration for effect, meant to suggest a large number. Martial ironically implies that dining with large numbers of people he doesn't know is dining alone. The name Fabullus here may have been suggested by poem 13 of Catullus, in which he invites his friend Fabullus to dinner.

11.37.  Martial hints that the rings that recently adorned the shins of Zoilus were the shackles of a slave, which makes his current show of wealth more unsuitable.

11.38.  Kay argues that twenty thousand sesterces was an unusually high price for an unskilled slave (152–53). A deaf driver of a carriage, however, would be desirable because he could not overhear the conversations of the occupants (Shackleton Bailey 3:35n). The Aulus addressed here is Martial's friend Aulus Pudens (3:378).

11.40.  Glycera is a common name for a prostitute (Kay 157); in this poem it is clear that she is a private mistress to Lupercus. Though Lupercus tells Aelianus he has not fucked her for a month, his explanation makes clear that he actually uses her only for oral sex.

11.42.  Hybla in Sicily (Shackleton Bailey 3:359) and Mount Hymettus in Greece (3:360) were both known for producing excellent honey, whereas the honey of Corsica was inferior (3:39n). *Cecropian* refers to King Cecrops of Attica, Greece (3:347). Kay hypothesizes that Martial was asked to extemporize verses (160–61).

11.43.  Martial is here pretending to have a wife for the sake of arguing with her about whether a wife can take the place of boys in her husband's sex life if she agrees to let him sodomize her. Using classical precedents of gods and heroes who slept with both women and boys, Martial proves that boys are preferred for sodomy. Jove (here called the Thunderer), married Juno and abducted the Trojan prince Ganymede to be his cupbearer and catamite. Hercules (born in Tiryns) married Megara, but also had sex with his pageboy Hylas. Phoebus unsuccessfully pursued Daphne, who turned into a tree to escape him, but he then fell in love with a Spartan boy, Hyacinthus, referred to as Oebalian (after Oebalius, a Spartan king who in some accounts was the father of Hyacinthus) (Shackleton Bailey 3:41n). In *The Iliad*, the hero Achilles, the grandson of Aeacus, is in love with his slave girl Briseis, but later traditions also portrayed him as being the lover of his friend Patroclus.

11.44. Martial says that the addressee of this poem was born when Lucius Junius Brutus was the Republic's first consul, circa 509 BCE (Kay 166). It is an obvious exaggeration for comic effect. As he often does, Martial here implies that legacy hunters would befriend rich old people without heirs, hoping to inherit their money.

11.45. Kay notes that brothels had cubicles that might be labeled with the name, sexual specialty, or price of the prostitute within, who could be male or female. The poem implies that Cantharus must be interested in oral sex or being buggered, since he is so eager to hide what he is doing (166–67).

11.46. Kay points out that this is one of several Martial epigrams (including 3.75 and 4.50) that suggest that fellatio is the best treatment for impotence in old men (170). He also suggests that Mevius may still be able to ejaculate (instead of just pissing) but cannot maintain an erection sufficient for sex or sodomy (169).

11.47. According to Kay, Pompey's portico was a spot frequented by prostitutes; prostitutes also were to be found at the temple of Isis, an Egyptian goddess identified with Io, the daughter of Inachus (171). Spartan wrestlers smeared their bodies with *ceroma*, "a muddy substance containing oil, coating the floor of a wrestling ring" (Shackleton Bailey 1:292n). The humor of the poem lies in the contrast between Lattara's seeming manliness, misogyny, and avoidance of sex and his actual performance of cunnilingus, which was considered shameful and effeminate. Kay observes that athletes would traditionally avoid sex so as not to weaken themselves competitively (172).

11.50. Silius Italicus was a consul under Nero in 68 CE and the author of *Punica*, a Latin epic on the Second Punic War (Shackleton Bailey 3:383). According to Pliny the Younger, Silius bought the rundown tomb of Vergil near Naples, which he restored and treated as a shrine (*Epistles* 3.7, cited in Kay 174). Posterity is far from considering Silius to be the poetic equal of Vergil, so Martial is exaggerating his talent as a compliment to a patron.

11.51. Lampsacus was a city on the Hellespont that was famous for its cult of Priapus, the fertility god endowed with a giant penis (Kay 102).

11.57. Marcus Severus was a literary man and a friend of Martial's (Shackleton Bailey 3:382). Martial is affecting embarrassment at sending a poem to a man who is a poet himself and is flattering him by comparing him to Jove. The ending literally says "If you don't want what you already have, what then will you accept?" (3:53).

11.60. Chione (Greek for "snowy") and Phlogis (Greek for "fiery") would both be prostitutes (Shackleton Bailey 3:55n). Both Priam and Pelias were known for living to be quite old. *Aluta* means "soft leather" and is here used to signify a limp penis (Kay 202). Shackleton Bailey mentions that Criton (a Greek name that suggests a male physician) has the kind of cure that Phlogis needs (i.e., sex), which Hygia (either the goddess of health or a female doctor) could not provide (3:55n). Martial is making one of his frequent jokes about male doctors having sex with female patients.

11.62. Lesbia's attempt to boast that she is in such demand that she never gives sex away is confirmed by Martial, but in a way she didn't intend. She never is fucked for free because she always has to pay, implying that she is old or ugly or both.

11.63. Philomusus is making insinuations about Martial's apparent preference for well-endowed catamites. Since a large penis would be moot in a boy who would be sodomized, he is suggesting that Martial prefers the passive role in sex (which was considered shameful among Roman men). According to Kay, Martial implies that just as the well-endowed statues of Priapus were meant to punish thieves in a garden by sodomizing them, so his well-endowed boys will punish Philomusus for asking nosy questions (209).

11.64. Faustus apparently boasts of writing to many girls, probably implying that he is propositioning them. Martial deflates him with the response that the girls don't write back. Kay notes that the Latin name Faustus, meaning *lucky*, is ironic in the context of this epigram (210).

11.66. Kay observes that all of the activities described could be lucrative, but were considered discreditable. Paid political informers had done well under Domitian, but were being punished under Nerva. The slanderers operated in the legal system; a *negotiator* could be either a pimp or a small trader. A *lanista* trained gladiators. The Latin name Vacerra means "a log or post" and implies that he is too stupid to make money from even the most lucrative activities (212–13).

11.67. Martial illustrates the strained relationship between a stingy rich man who encourages a legacy hunter without giving him anything and the legacy hunter (here Martial himself) who eagerly hopes for the death of the man in order to gain something for his attentions.

11.68.  As someone who often asked for favors from important men, Martial himself would have had experience with the shame of being turned down.

11.71.  The name Leda was probably chosen for the wife because the Leda of myth also made her husband a cuckold, though, in that case, because she was raped by Jove. The Leda of this epigram is feigning hysteria to induce her impotent old husband to allow her to sleep with others as "therapy." According to Kay, Roman medicine did hold that hysteria was caused by lack of sex (222–23). Female doctors were common because male doctors were often rumored to have sex with female patients (224).

11.72.  Literally the second line says "compared to him Priapus is a eunuch." Priapus, the guardian god of gardens, is always portrayed as having a giant penis. Kay argues that Natta's calling the athlete's cock by a child's word for "penis" and being attracted by its size suggest that Natta is a fellator (224).

11.75.  Kay points out that both singers and athletes would often wear a *fibula*, an iron ring, on their foreskin to prevent or discourage sex, with the goal of preserving their voice or athletic prowess (229). Since Caelia's slave does not appear to be a singer, the fibula (which seems to be hiding the whole penis in this case) suggests that she is too modest to look at a penis. But if she is in public baths with other men, that seems to imply that she thinks they don't have penises worth looking at. Martial suggests that she is actually hiding her slave's attractions from the public and that she may be sleeping with him herself. To prove that she isn't begrudging the others from ogling the slave, she must expose him to view.

11.76.  Paetus, who has loaned Martial ten thousand sesterces and Bucco two hundred thousand, uses Bucco's default as an excuse to call in his smaller loan to Martial. Martial jokes that he shouldn't be made to pay for someone else's misdeeds; if Paetus can afford to lose two hundred thousand, he can afford to lose another ten thousand.

11.77.  Vacerra sits in public toilets all over town in the hope of meeting someone who will invite him to dinner. The implication is that he cannot afford to feed himself, like Philo in Martial's 5.47. Because the privies were large rooms with many-holed benches, they were places where one would tend to meet others.

11.79.  Martial has reached the first milestone at the tenth hour and is therefore an hour late to dinner (Shackleton Bailey 3:67n) Accused of arriving late because of laziness, he counters that the mules that pulled the carriage Paetus sent to bring him to dinner were the cause of his lateness. Though it might seem cheeky to blame his host, Martial is trying to amuse through a surprising response and the resourcefulness of his blame-passing.

11.81.   Kay observes that the Greek name Aegle, meaning "splendor," would be suitable for a prostitute (239) and that Dindymus is a suitable name for a eunuch (239) because it is the name of a mountain associated with the cult of Cybele, whose priests were eunuchs (74). The girl is lying in bed between a eunuch and an old man, neither of whom is capable of sex, though both keep trying. She therefore calls on Venus to solve the problems of all three by giving the two men what they lack.

11.83.   Sosibianus makes his profit when his "guests" die and leave him all their money (Shackleton Bailey 3:71n).

11.85.   Literally, Zoilus has been struck "by a star" (Shackleton Bailey 3:73n). According to Kay, the Romans believed that the influence of the stars and planets could cause paralysis (246). Because his tongue has been paralyzed, Zoilus will be forced to abandon cunnilingus (considered a shameful practice by the Romans) for conventional intercourse.

11.86.   Parthenopaeus was a common name for a slave (Kay 247). The treatment of his cough is so appealing that the slave has no desire to recover.

11.87.   Charidemus, who prefers sodomy, is forced by poverty to court old women in order to support himself. Martial typically presents sex with an old woman as a fate worse than death.

11.88.   Carisianus unintentionally reveals that he allows himself to be sodomized when he says that diarrhea is keeping him from sodomizing (Shackleton Bailey 3:73n). Though to sodomize was not considered objectionable, to be penetrated was always shameful for a man. Because he is the addressee of the poem and not its target, the Lupus mentioned here is probably a friend of Martial's (Kay 249).

11.89.   Floral garlands were a common gift between friends (as in 9.60) or lovers (Kay 249). Here Martial implies that the fact that the garland had rested on Polla's head first would make it dearer than an untouched garland.

11.92.   Martial consistently uses the name Zoilus for an evil person.

11.93.   As Kay points out, the melodramatic and high-flown language is exaggerated for ironic effect; the poet's name, which means "God's gift," is clearly sarcastic (257).

11.96.   The fountain is a pool fed by the Marcian aqueduct (Shackleton Bailey 3:78n). Martial implies that, though both are slaves, the "citizen" page should have precedence over the adult German conquered in foreign wars (3:79n). Both dislike of foreigners and sexual interest in the boy may have played a role in Martial's response.

11.97. This poem could be a sexual boast combined with an insult to an unappealing woman, or a case of blame-passing for impotence, as in 6.23. Kay mentions that the Greek name Telesilla (which means "little fulfillment") may suggest that the woman is no good in bed (264).

11.99. The Symplegades, also known as the Cyanean Rocks, were two legendary rocks at the entrance to the Black Sea, which would clash together, destroying any ship that tried to pass between them (Shackleton Bailey 3:350).

11.101. Kay observes that Thais, the name of a famous courtesan of Alexander the Great, was in frequent use for prostitutes. Exaggerated comparisons making fun of thinness were common among Greek writers (272). Flaccus, a wealthy friend of Martial's, is often addressed in his epigrams (Shackleton Bailey 3:355).

11.102. Aediles were officials who were charged with reporting all prodigies (Shackleton Bailey 3:83n).

11.103. The Safronius mentioned here is Safronius Rufus of 4.71 (Shackleton Bailey 3:380). He must have been a close enough friend of Martial's to be willing to take good-natured ribbing, since Martial uses pseudonyms for his less flattering attacks (Kay 276).

11.105. Though only the weight and not the nature of the gift is specified, Kay hypothesizes that the gift was probably an item made of silver, due to the similarity of this epigram to others that describe gifts of silver by weight (283–84). Shackleton Bailey notes that the joke is based on the assumption that previous gifts have created an expectation that Garricus "owes" at least as much in subsequent gifts (3:87n).

11.106. Vibius Maximus was a high-ranking military officer (Shackleton Bailey 3:389), who later became the governor of Egypt (Kay 284–85). Martial shows his self-deprecating humor by implying that his poem isn't worth reading, while gently poking fun at a man too busy to read a short epigram.

11.108. Martial is reminding his readers that he has bills to pay and that if they want more poems from him, they need to help him financially. As Kay points out, the Latin name Lupus (meaning "wolf") is an appropriate name for an insistent creditor. This reminder of financial obligation on the part of readers might fit someone whom Martial has flattered in his poems, but is humorously inappropriate when directed at readers in general (286).

## Book Twelve

12.7. This epigram, like 11.101, belongs to the tradition of humor through exaggerated comparisons and ridicule of unattractive physical features.

12.9.   Cornelius Palma was consul in 99 CE (Shackleton Bailey 3:372). Trajan, who had been born in Italica, near what is now Seville, had become emperor in January 98 CE (3:97–98n). Around 98 CE, Martial returned to his hometown of Bilbilis in northeastern Spain, where he spent the rest of his life (Howell, *Martial* 26).

12.10.   Martial focuses on the irony that Africanus, who owns a hundred million already, is still looking for more in the form of legacies from others.

12.12.   This epigram suggests a solution to a situation Martial must often have encountered, in which people make generous promises to him when they are drunk that they "forget" once they are sober.

12.13.   Because Martial was dependent on the generosity of rich men, he must have suffered often from their caprices and piques. This poem is addressed to Pompeius Auctus, a legal expert and friend of Martial's (Shackleton Bailey 3:377).

12.16.   The slaves Labienus bought are catamites, so Martial is using "plow" in a sexual sense.

12.17.   The name Dama was often used for slaves (Shackleton Bailey 3:351), so in this poem it suggests a slave or poor freedman (3:103n). The wines named in this poem are all excellent ones, and the foods are also luxury items.

12.18.   The Juvenal mentioned here is probably Decimus Junius Juvenalis, the famous satirist, who was Martial's friend (Shackleton Bailey 3:361). Martial seems to be reminding Juvenal of the onerous duties of visiting patrons in order to contrast them with the pleasures of his rustic life of retirement in Bilbilis in northeastern Spain, the town of his birth, which was populated by Celtiberians (Spanish Celts). The Subura was a bustling section of Rome. Diana's hill is the Aventine, which had a temple to Diana (3:105n). Boterdus was a sacred wood near Bilbilis (3:343), and Platea was another local place (3:376).

12.20.   Martial is using "has" to mean "has sex with" (Shackleton Bailey 3:107n).

12.22.   Physical defects are frequent targets of Martial's humor.

12.23.   As in 12.22, 3.8, 3.39, and other epigrams, Martial makes fun of a person with just one eye.

12.26.   The bandits may be implying that Saenia was too ugly to fuck or, as Shackleton Bailey suggests, that she performed other sexual acts (3:110n).

12.27.   Though Martial complains when he, as a guest, is served different wine than his host is drinking (3.49, 4.85), he justifies serving a cheaper wine to Cinna because Cinna drinks so much.

12.30.  A sober slave would be unlikely to be sneaking into the wine, but friends would typically be drinking together, so a sober man in the crowd might put a damper on the fun.

12.31.  Martial is describing his home in Bilbilis, after he retired to Hispania. Marcella was his local patroness. Nausicaa is a Phaeacian princess in *The Odyssey*, whose father Alcinous has gardens described as a sort of earthly paradise, in which fruits are always in season.

12.34.  This poem, addressed to Martial's closest friend, Lucius Julius Martialis (Shackleton Bailey 3:361), looks back fondly on their years together in Rome. Martial was living in retirement in Spain when he wrote it.

12.35.  To Romans, there were more shameful things than being sodomized. Martial implies that Callistratus also performs oral sex.

12.40.  The one thing that Pontilianus does without Martial is not specified, but is implied to be something sexual of a discreditable nature. Martial casts himself as a long-suffering legacy hunter, willing to commit any hypocrisy to keep the rich target happy, but his true feelings are revealed in his wish that Pontilianus will die soon.

12.42.  Though sexual liaisons between grown men and boys were accepted by Roman society, the idea of two adult men wanting to marry one another would have seemed absurd, and the idea of a bearded man wearing the wedding veil of a virgin was even more ridiculous.

12.45.  This early form of a toupee, made from kidskin (presumably with the hair still on it) excites derision from Martial, who also makes fun of Phoebus for painting hair on his bald head in 6.57.

12.46.  This poem is probably addressed to one of Martial's slave boys, given his other similar poems about their uncooperative behavior.

12.47.  Martial implies that the ones who buy verse by Lupercus and Gallus are the true madmen.

12.51.  Aulus Pudens is a friend of Martial's and is frequently addressed in his poems (Shackleton Bailey 3:378).

12.56.  When people recovered from illness, their friends would send them *soteria*, gifts to congratulate them on their recovery (Shackleton Bailey 3:137n). Polycharmus seems to be faking frequent illness to collect these gifts.

12.58.  Alauda's wife, knowing that he sleeps with slave girls, indulges in sex with the slaves who carry her litter. Though the double standard of Roman times endorses Alauda's infidelity, not hers, Martial implies that the two deserve one another.

12.61.  According to Martial, Ligurra longs to be considered important enough to be lampooned by him, pretending to fear such notoriety, but actually desiring it. Martial says Ligurra is unworthy of his own verses, but fit for those of scurrilous graffiti writers who scrawl their work in latrines, brothels, and other dark corners. The drunk bard may be living under an archway, as homeless people do even now, though it is possible that he chooses such a location to write in so that he will be less likely to be caught in the act.

12.64. Cinna, Martial implies, has no taste for beauty, only for food.

12.65. Phyllis, ironically, asks for far less than Martial is prepared to give for the night of sex with her, and by asking first, she loses out on what he would have given. Prostitutes usually charged more for sexual services such as anal or oral intercourse than for regular intercourse, so her moderate demands are surprising.

12.69. Martial implies that the friends are as phony as Paulus' "antique" paintings and wine cups (Shackleton Bailey 3:150n).

12.71. Martial suggests that Lygdus formerly satisfied even requests that *should* be refused, such as a request for fellatio (Shackleton Bailey 3:151n). A similar point is made about Thais in 4.12.

12.73. The last line means "I won't believe it unless I read it, Catullus" (Shackleton Bailey 3:153). Since the will of Catullus would not be read until after his death, Shackleton Bailey takes this to be a hint to Catullus to die (3:152n). Since Martial frequently praises the poet Catullus (ca. 84–ca. 54 BCE) and seeks to imitate him, there may also be a self-deprecating allusion here to Martial's hope that he will be seen as the heir of that Catullus.

12.76. Though the farmer has more food and wine than he can consume, he can get no money for them (Shackleton Bailey 3:155n). The *as*, here translated as "cent," was a bronze coin of low value.

12.78. Shackleton Bailey notes that plaintiffs could challenge defendants in law cases to swear an oath that their claims were true; to refuse to swear was an admission of guilt. Martial would rather pay damages than admit the truth that he has not written anything against Bithynicus, implying that he wishes he had (3:157n).

12.79. As in 12.71 and 4.12, the joke is that anyone who refuses no requests will agree to perform fellatio.

12.80. Martial often, as here, shows disgust at the praise of poets he considers unworthy, perhaps feeling that his own poetry was undervalued by comparison.

12.81. Though the pun on *alicula* (light coat) and *alica* (a drink made from spelt, a kind of grain) cannot be preserved in English, the irony of

Umber's sending a more expensive gift when he was poor than after he becomes rich is still clear. Umber sent a costlier gift when he was poor because he hoped to gain something from Martial. Once he was rich himself, he had no incentive to stay in Martial's favor.

12.84.  According to myth, Pelops had a shoulder of ivory because his father Tantalus had killed him and served him as a meal to the gods. All of the gods refrained from eating any of the cannibalistic feast except Demeter, who was so distracted by grief for her daughter Persephone's recent kidnapping that she ate his left shoulder. When the gods brought the boy back to life, the missing shoulder was supplied by an ivory substitute. Polytimus, a slave of Martial's, longs to cut his hair as a sign of manhood and an end to his role as Martial's catamite. Martial does not want to grant that wish, but once he does, he finds Polytimus even more attractive with his hair cut short, like a bridegroom's, revealing his ivory shoulders.

12.85.  Martial may have associated the name Fabullus with smelling because of poem 13 of Catullus, in which Catullus tells Fabullus that once he has smelled the perfume of the girlfriend of Catullus, he will wish he were all nose. Martial makes his usual joke about oral sex causing bad breath.

12.86.  Martial not only points out the irony of owning many desirable slaves while being unable to perform sexually, but also hints that the only sexual options available to such a person were the shameful ones of performing oral sex or being sodomized.

12.87.  People reclined barefoot on couches while dining (Shackleton Bailey 3:163n), so Cotta would have left his sandals in his slave's care. Since the slave has twice lost the sandals and Cotta has no other slave he can bring, he solves the problem by going to dinner barefoot.

12.91.  Magulla shares not only her husband's bed, but also his male bedmate. She does not share the good-looking boy who pours his wine (and who may also be his catamite). Her reason may be either that the husband is more jealous of that boy and might be tempted to poison her if she had sex with him or that having her wine poured by her husband's darling gives him a greater opportunity to poison her.

12.92.  Martial implies that it is as likely that he will get wealth and power as it is that Priscus will become a lion.

12.93.  The dwarf that Labulla keeps as a fool is compared to her own husband (a bigger fool) in that she is able to carry on her adultery right under his nose without his suspecting a thing.

12.95.  The books of Sybaris were well-known pornographic works by Hemitheon, called "The Sybarite," though Mussetius is otherwise unknown (Shackleton Bailey 3:167n). Sullivan points out that Martial tends to portray masturbation as an inferior mode of sexual activity (190–91).

12.96.  Here, as in 11.43, Martial makes the argument that wives should not consider boys to be their rivals and should not try to compete with the boys by allowing the husband to sodomize them; this poem, however, is addressed to an unnamed woman instead of to Martial's invented wife, as it was in 11.43.

12.97.  Martial here writes to Bassus as if in the capacity of a lawyer for the neglected wife of Bassus, to shame him into fulfilling his marital obligations to her. Though Martial himself was averse to marrying and often has negative things to say about wives and marriage, he supports the expectation that married men would make an effort to reproduce with their wives.

# Bibliography

Freud, Sigmund. *Jokes and Their Relation to the Unconscious*. Translated and edited by James Strachey. London: Routledge and Kegan Paul, 1960. Originally published as *Der Witz und seine Beziehung zum Unbewussten* (Vienna: F. Deuticke, 1905).

Galán Vioque, Guillermo. *Martial, Book VII: A Commentary*. Translated by J. J. Zoltowski. Boston: Brill, 2002.

Henriksén, Christer. *A Commentary on Martial, Epigrams Book 9*. Oxford: Oxford University Press, 2012.

Howell, Peter. *A Commentary on Book One of the Epigrams of Martial*. London: Athlone, 1980.

———. *Martial*. London: Bristol Classical, 2009.

———. *Martial: Epigrams V*. Warminster, UK: Aris & Phillips, 1995.

Kay, N. M. *Martial Book XI: A Commentary*. London: Duckworth, 1985.

Moreno Soldevila, Rosario. *Martial, Book IV: A Commentary*. Boston: Brill, 2006.

Pliny. *Letters and Panegyricus, Books 1–7*. Vol. 1. Translated by Betty Radice. Cambridge, MA: Harvard University Press, 1969.

Richlin, Amy. *The Garden of Priapus: Sexuality and Aggression in Roman Humor*. Rev. ed. New York: Oxford University Press, 1992.

———. "The Meaning of *Irrumare* in Catullus and Martial." *Classical Philology* 76 (1981): 40–46.

Shackleton Bailey, D. R., ed. and trans. *Martial: Epigrams*. 3 vols. Cambridge, MA: Harvard University Press, 1993.

Spisak, Art L. *Martial: A Social Guide*. London: Duckworth, 2007.

Sullivan, J. P. *Martial: The Unexpected Classic*. New York: Cambridge University Press, 1991.

# Bibliography

Williams, Craig A. *Martial: Epigrams Book Two*. New York: Oxford University Press, 2004.

# Index

# Wisconsin Studies in Classics

*Series Editors*

Patricia A. Rosenmeyer, Laura McClure, and
Mark Stansbury-O'Donnell

---

E. A. Thompson
*Romans and Barbarians: The Decline of the Western Empire*

H. I. Marrou
*A History of Education in Antiquity*
*Histoire de l'Education dans l'Antiquité,*
    translated by **George Lamb**

Jennifer Tolbert Roberts
*Accountability in Athenian Government*

Erika Simon
*Festivals of Attica: An Archaeological Commentary*

Warren G. Moon, editor
*Ancient Greek Art and Iconography*

G. Michael Woloch
*Roman Cities: Les villes romaines* by **Pierre Grimal**,
    translated and edited by **G. Michael Woloch**,
    together with A Descriptive Catalogue of Roman Cities by
    **G. Michael Woloch**

**Rudolf Blum**
**Hans H. Wellisch,** translator
*Kallimachos: The Alexandrian Library and the Origins of
    Bibliography*

**David Castriota**
*Myth, Ethos, and Actuality: Official Art in Fifth Century B.C. Athens*

**Barbara Hughes Fowler,** editor and translator
*Archaic Greek Poetry: An Anthology*

**John H. Oakley** and **Rebecca H. Sinos**
*The Wedding in Ancient Athens*

**Richard Daniel De Puma** and **Jocelyn Penny Small,** editors
*Murlo and the Etruscans: Art and Society in Ancient Etruria*

**Judith Lynn Sebesta** and **Larissa Bonfante,** editors
*The World of Roman Costume*

**Jennifer Larson**
*Greek Heroine Cults*

**Warren G. Moon,** editor
*Polykleitos, the Doryphoros, and Tradition*

**Paul Plass**
*The Game of Death in Ancient Rome: Arena Sport and
    Political Suicide*

**Margaret S. Drower**
*Flinders Petrie: A Life in Archaeology*

**Susan B. Matheson**
*Polygnotos and Vase Painting in Classical Athens*

**Jenifer Neils,** editor
*Worshipping Athena: Panathenaia and Parthenon*

Sinclair Bell and Helen Nagy, editors
*New Perspectives on Etruria and Early Rome*

Barbara Pavlock
*The Image of the Poet in Ovid's "Metamorphoses"*

Paul Cartledge and Fiona Rose Greenland, editors
*Responses to Oliver Stone's "Alexander": Film, History, and
   Cultural Studies*

Amalia Avramidou
*The Codrus Painter: Iconography and Reception of Athenian Vases
   in the Age of Pericles*

Shane Butler
*The Matter of the Page: Essays in Search of Ancient and
   Medieval Authors*

Allison Glazebrook and Madeleine Henry, editors
*Greek Prostitutes in the Ancient Mediterranean, 800 BCE–200 CE*

Norman Austin
*Sophocles' "Philoctetes" and the Great Soul Robbery*

Sophocles
A verse translation by David Mulroy, with introduction and notes
*Oedipus Rex*

John Andreau and Raymond Descat
*The Slave in Greece and Rome*
*Esclave en Grèce et à Rome*, translated by Marion Leopold

Amanda Wilcox
*The Gift of Correspondence in Classical Rome: Friendship in Cicero's
   "Ad Familiares" and Seneca's "Moral Epistles"*

Mark Buchan
*Perfidy and Passion: Reintroducing the "Iliad"*

**Sophocles**
A verse translation by **David Mulroy,** with introduction and notes
*Antigone*

**Geoffrey W. Bakewell**
*Aeschylus's "Suppliant Women": The Tragedy of Immigration*

**Elizabeth Paulette Baughan**
*Couched in Death: "Klinai" and Identity in Anatolia and Beyond*

**Benjamin Eldon Stevens**
*Silence in Catullus*

**Horace**
Translated with commentary by **David R. Slavitt**
*Odes*

**Martial**
Translated with notes by **Susan McLean**
*Selected Epigrams*

**Mary B. Hollinshead**
*Shaping Ceremony: Monumental Steps and Greek Architecture*

**Ovid**
A verse translation by **Julia Dyson Hejduk,** with introduction and notes
*The Offense of Love: "Ars Amatoria," "Remedia Amoris," and "Tristia" 2*

**Sophocles**
A verse translation by **David Mulroy,** with introduction and notes
*Oedipus at Colonus*